Heart & Soul

Living a Love-Filled, Spirit-Guided,
Consciously-Created Life

Powerful You!
PUBLISHING
Sharing Wisdom ~ Shining Light

HEART & SOUL
Living a Love-Filled, Spirit-Guided,
Consciously-Created Life

The authors of this book do not dispense medical advice or prescribe the use of any technique as a form of treatment for physical, emotional, or medical problems without the advice of a physician, either directly or indirectly. Nor is this book intended to provide personalized legal, accounting, financial, or investment advice. Readers are encouraged to seek the counsel of competent professionals with regards to such matters. The intent of the authors is to provide general information to individuals who are taking positive steps in their lives for emotional and spiritual well-being. If you use any of the information in this book for yourself, which is your constitutional right, the authors and the publisher assume no responsibility for your actions.

Published by: Powerful You! Inc. USA
powerfulyoupublishing.com

Library of Congress Control Number: 2018911106

Sue Urda and Kathy Fyler – First Edition

ISBN: 978-1-7328128-0-2

First Edition November 2018

Self Help / Women's Studies

Printed in the United States of America

Dedication

*This book is dedicated to those willing
to search their souls and follow their hearts.
May your path be enlightening and
your lessons be expansive.*

Table of Contents

Foreword

Have you ever stopped to ponder the questions, "What's it *all* about" or "Who am I?" If so, you are in synch with a few other billion Souls walking this earth, each seeking to find meaning and fulfillment and of course, self-worth. In fact, these are age-old questions that have been contemplated from the beginning of recorded time. Wouldn't you think that perhaps the answer should have been found by now? Isn't it time? As you contemplate these questions do you have answers that come to you? For most, the answers are still a part of their quest but what if what's true for me is also true for you? Or, that the purpose of the question is just to initiate the quest?

What if this one premise is true for each of us? ...

> ***The meaning of life is to find you;***
> ***and finding you, gives life its meaning.***

The powerful messages of the stories in, *Heart and Soul*, would appear to hold that premise as true. Each of these women journeyed, some through the dark nights of their Soul, and found themselves redirected with new meaning for their lives as well. As they discovered their truths they re-discovered the light of their Souls and the purpose of that light to—illuminate and clarify their wisdom and inner-sight.

Like they, are you willing to ask these questions and do what it takes to find those answers? If so, perhaps allow them to inspire you, follow their lead, be bold enough to ask; who are you? What are you doing here? Why would finding *you* be so important? What could be the reward? Why? Because in everything you do, *you are* reflected right back to you. Like clues in a scavenger hunt, they lead you to 'the promised land' of getting in touch; really knowing who you are, what you are meant to do and how you will be fulfilled. What could be more important than collecting all these lost parts of you?

What could be so compelling about this game you might ask? Why continue with this insatiable hunt when there are so many other things calling to you that are way more fun! The answer is quite clear; and it's probably why you're right here! You can't help yourself! You continue to explore you, because seeking to know your Self is hardwired within you and every little peek or glimmer you get of the luminous you, absolutely delights and enchants you. Did you ever realize that? You cannot resist your own light!

So, if this could be your purpose here, what of the world around you? What if, every aspect of the design of you, as well as that of 'The Universe' has been created to aid in *your* Self-discovery too? What if everything you are experiencing is conspiring at this very moment for *your* one *AHA* moment, your personal epiphany of remembering who you really are? How would that knowledge change the way you live and the way you are?

I have often said that every experience reflects to us who we are in that moment. Like a snapshot, it reflects our thoughts, our beliefs, our desires, and perhaps most importantly, it reflects what's accumulated around our heart. Could this imply that there is indeed purpose in our lives, as well as purpose to each of our experiences too? What could that be you might ask? What's so important about *you*? Perhaps to help you remember who you are. But perhaps also so you can BE all you are meant to be and gift this world with the gifts of *you*, the real, '*Powerful You.*' That rings true for me, does it you? After all, what greater evidence could there be than every human pursuing the same dream?

As you will witness, and what sets these remarkable women apart, is that not one of their journeys was for the weak of heart. It was arduous at times and called forward the parts of them that had been kept hidden and underdeveloped or even denied. Yet, those very parts gave them strength needed to move forward and "Become" whole once again as they had been from the start. Some of them traveled down roads that were quite scary, but as you will read, it appears their promise shared is that Self-Actualization will happen for you just as it happened for them. There will be no more important journey you can ever make as you align with your Heart and Soul and embrace your destiny, not only your fate.

As you read these beautiful stories in this heartwarming and inspiring book, you will be treated to more evidence that this journey for each is real; as is its relentless pursuit of the real you. This incredible cast of women have bared their Hearts and Souls; shared their journeys and stories so that you can witness the miracles that occur when the Call for Love is answered in the only way worthy; with courage to practice profound Self-Love. Their amazing commitment in this practice has delivered them to where they are today and their stories invite you to do the same. These women are Souls who said, "Yes" to their *becoming;* transforming their own lives and now inspiring the lives of others too; others just like me and just like you. This sharing of the real Self is the full measure of how transformation works.

There are those who may even say that they have been reborn. From my perspective, there is much more. Transformation occurred when they journeyed out of the fear in their heads and into trusting their hearts instead. They finally freed all that was within them all along by letting go of what had kept them weak and chose to be strong. So perhaps new life is not the result of a rebirth, but rather energy shapeshifted into a brand new form. The stretch and pull of their Heart and Soul brought back the memories of loving and living 'in the fold.' I know that comforts me, and I hope it does for you too, as we are reminded that we never walk this path alone.

So how does this happen? What is the catalyst that creates such profound change? Saying YES! With every shift into an aspect of you in alignment with your true nature, you are made anew. Never to be the same, never to replicate what or who you thought you were. It is impossible to return. Your new eyes, your new level of consciousness, your new Being is the result of an energy field that has never before been created. That's how profound the effects of change can be and as you will read, there is nothing about it that is limiting. It affects every aspect of life; every thought, every relationship, and every opportunity that follows. It is a brand new vibrational force that has real power and *calls* to the new possibilities of life to follow.

As you will see with the authors here, it was the power of their free will that was the catalyst for change, and their message to you is that you can do the same. You also have the capability and capacity to initiate change and see it through … to BE the change. The tenacity to do that is the journey of Self Love, the journey of the Heart and Soul aligned with all that you are; Divine Love.

What then should we think of these life experiences that bring us to our knees, wring us inside out, and stare us down with eyes of green? How many times would you face your own demons if you knew they had only one intent; to create a bridge from where you are, to where you are meant instead?

This is the journey captured so beautifully by Sue and Kathy, of Powerful You! Publishing in this inspirational anthology. They have done an incredible job gathering these courageous Souls who are here to share their extraordinary stories as well as the great wisdom and gifts they are now in touch with and free to share. You will see through their new eyes, hear through their new ears, and recognize the new sound of their voices. You will feel their Heart*Shifts* through new connections to their Heart and Soul, and their love shining through with more stories to be told. Thank you,

Kathy and Sue for providing this platform and holding the energy that has carried these valuable lessons through, reminding us of home. We the readers are blessed by all of you!

With Hugs, Healing, and Heart*Shifts*,
Marcy Neumann, The Heart*Shift* Coach
HeartShiftCoach.com

Introduction

Sharing your story is risky.
Some will be moved, others will disapprove,
And some simply won't understand.
And when you choose to do it from your heart and soul,
despite what others think, you risk moving mountains.

Storytelling is and art and a calling. It is also a gift, a contribution, a love letter to the world. This book and these authors are no exception.

Most authors came forth already open and willing to go to the depths of their personal journeys. They knew their stories could change the hearts, minds, and even the lives of readers. Others came to their stories 'kicking and screaming'--even though, of course, they made the decision to open their hearts. Interestingly, those who fought themselves the hardest along the way to painstakingly bare their souls are now content in the knowledge that they stepped forward from their inner self and unleashed their heart for the higher good, knowing that if one soul is touched the fear and deep inner work of writing is well worth it.

The simple act of stepping into the work and allowing oneself to be vulnerable provides healing for the heart and soul.

And so, herein lie the hearts and souls of 24 incredible women. Some of them had no idea that they were writers until the title of this book and the opportunity to collaborate called to them. They were drawn by some compelling force to open to the truth of themselves. Now, on the other side of the writing process, they will tell you that they have put forth not only their hearts and souls, they also reveal the essence of some very important aspects of their lives.

When you are called to share your story, there's nothing that will stop you; not fear, not angst, not lack of confidence, not the monkey mind, and certainly not the voice of anyone else. The call, the pull, is so great that it must be answered. It's as if the choice is not really yours... although of course, the calling is your own inner voice and it must be affirmatively answered.

In talking with each of the authors, we know that the overwhelming reason and decision to write their story was to help someone else who is searching for answers, someone who needs encouragement and a light shone on the path before them. Many tell of the ecstasy of their transformation or the happy story of how things can work out beautifully no matter the starting point. Others share secrets that they have guarded for many years and, for the first time, emerge from their silence because of the opening, opportunity, and healing that comes along with it. No matter their reason, they each decided the time to share her story is now.

What they all discovered is that an energetic transformation occurs when one puts pen to paper (or fingers to the keypad) with the intent to reveal her truth. As you read each story in this book, you will find yourself feeling the very core of the emotion of each author, whether she is speaking of creating or expanding a business, healing from some sort of tragedy, trauma, or abuse in her life, opening to her inborn gifts and talents, or she is still finding her way to living from her heart and soul.

Each transformation is unique and holds its own gifts.

Heart & Soul. If you are drawn to the title of this book, you are undoubtedly on your own journey of awakening to a more conscious way of being. You are ready to step more fully into your power and, in fact, by picking up this book, you're already doing it. You have already leaped ahead towards your destination and, as you flip through the pages and read the words, you will catapult yourself even further along this path. Why? Because we are all connected, and your desire and willingness cannot help but move you forward. The only question is; will you go forth *with ease?*

Are you ready and willing to live from your heart and soul? We believe you are.

Our wish for you is that you commit to yourself to be aware of your calling, your purpose, your joy. Delve into your heart, listen to your inner voice, answer the calling of your soul's purpose—however great or quiet, wherever it shows up, and whatever or whoever is the bearer. Be faithful to your desire to live in and from your heart space. As you do this, you will find your life to be more filled with love, more guided by Spirit, and more consciously aligned with your own heart and soul.

With deep gratitude and love,
Sue Urda & Kathy Fyler
Powerful You! Inc.

Open Your Heart & Soul.

Embrace the
Beauty of You.

Feeding My Sensitive Soul
Tiffany Guske

It was the fall of 2000, and I had everything an aspiring yuppie could want—a downtown high-rise with a doorman and a Lake Michigan view, a new job in a skyscraper office with cherry wood furniture and a high-back leather chair, the finest entertainment and cuisine at my fingertips every night of the week, a freshly framed graduate diploma, a husband I adored, and the knowledge there was so much more to come. I had arrived. *Or so I thought.*

I was working for KPMG LLP, one of the Big 5 accounting firms, leading the Human Resources function for the Midwest Region. The job was beyond my experience level when I first took it, which only made it more attractive. Driven by the billable hour, the dog-eat-dog culture demanded long hours and personal sacrifice, and I was determined to prove to them, the world, and myself that I deserved to be there.

When you're part of the Big 5, you're always on the lookout to steal competitor talent and clients. So when Arthur Andersen, a top-of-the-food-chain accounting and audit firm, tumbled to the ground as part of the Enron scandal in the summer of 2002, the remaining Big 4 attacked like frenzied sharks. Arthur Andersen had a thriving office in Kansas City, and suddenly I found myself in charge of managing the potential acquisition. It didn't matter that I lacked the background experience to execute this, nor that we didn't have enough people to get the job done; I was determined to succeed, no matter what it took.

What followed were eighteen-hour days of fire-drill integration, complex legal challenges, and battles with Arthur Andersen partners who fought to hold onto the culture and organization they had once known.

My ego wants me to tell you that we acquired the entire existing office—all partners, employees, and clients; my *spirit,* however, wants me to share a different perspective. During this six-week period, I pushed myself mentally and physically far beyond what was reasonable and rational. Taking a breather or asking for help were not options. It would mean admitting to the world, "Hey, everyone—I'm not perfect!"—which after all my hard work, I was unwilling to do.

The physical breakdown came soon after the close of the deal. While the acquisition was *technically* complete, the tempo hadn't slowed for me or my team. There were also the heartache and headaches of layoffs typical of nearly every acquisition, meaning I now had to dismiss people with whom I had just been in the trenches. Yet despite being in full-shutdown mode I pressed on, determined to prove to everyone that I was indestructible, even if that meant stepping out of meetings to vomit in the restroom and returning as if nothing had happened. I was still working fourteen-hour-plus days, not allowing my body the sleep it desperately needed and, worst of all, demanding that others behave in the same self-destructive manner. Looking back, I know I wasn't my most productive, effective, or caring self, but that is tough to acknowledge when you are nothing more than a shell. So with the grace and timing that only the Divine can facilitate, my physical body said "Sorry, Tiff, you and I aren't going to do this anymore."

Two weeks after the deal closed, my husband made the urgent call to Dr. Edelberg, my internist who specialized in integrative medicine. For days he had witnessed my struggle to walk to the bathroom, my inability to keep down fluids or food, and increasingly intense aches and pains. The next thing I knew we were in the car, headed to his clinic.

Dr. Edelberg understood my sensitive nature and what I needed in order to restore my body and spirit. But even then I was not giving up without a fight, arguing with him about returning to work even while hooked up to an IV drip. The gravity of my situation began to hit me when my doctor turned away and instead addressed my husband. By that afternoon, I was put on indefinite medical leave, which provided simultaneously a sense of relief and nothing short of sheer panic.

All told, I required more than two months of medical treatment, focusing on rest, hydration, and nutrition. But it soon became clear that ending the dysfunctional drive for perfection and people-pleasing that had taken me down this path would require a longer-term solution. As an empath and intuitive, I'd struggled my entire life to untangle my emotions from the emotions of others. I could feel everything, all the time, in an incredibly heightened manner. This combination of constantly striving for achievement and hypersensitivity was beyond exhausting. And while I didn't yet have a label for it, over the next few months I would come to understand that I indeed was a "highly sensitive person" (HSP), and that I needed help.

Although intensive psychotherapy was a logical addition to my treatment, I would soon find that my therapist had a bigger transformation in mind. He sought to teach me *mindfulness skills and techniques* that would not only facilitate my healing process, but also alter my way of being. Walking this path allowed me to gently shed my old habits of thinking, creating a freedom I'd never felt. The most significant and impactful of these practices was qigong, an ancient Chinese approach to health that integrates physical postures, breathing techniques, and focused intention. This was the practice that would jump-start the connection to my spirit by guiding me to quiet my mind and be present. It brought me a sense of calm, focus, and clarity unlike anything I had experienced before. I found myself craving this time of practice, and realized that this sacred connection to the deepest part of myself, my spirit, was what had been missing all along.

I'd assumed the changes that nurtured my spirit and sensitivities would be enough to support my career path in corporate, but I continually felt myself being tugged back into old patterns. The truth was, this particular environment would always be a challenge for an HSP, so I set off to find a better fit.

Pursuing a doctorate in psychology seemed a logical choice. I'd engaged in psychotherapy several times in my life and was a big believer in its ability to promote growth and healing. It was also a safe way for me to pursue a path of service without sacrificing my ego. After all, who could criticize the pursuit of a doctoral degree?

Life as a student had always fit like a glove. I settled back into it with ease and with the belief that I was accomplishing something that would both help others and provide me with a stable future and income. But after completing the required coursework, beginning my dissertation, and finishing my first internship the harsh realization set in that this profession would also challenge *my sensitive soul*. While my heart literally ached to help others, I found that working with mental illness was exhausting and draining. My days ended with feelings of depression and I never knew whether the feelings belonged to me or my clients. Even with the addition of new spiritual practices such as journaling, automatic writing, prayer and the use of Divination tools such as runes and angel cards, I couldn't seem to find a sense of peace and belonging.

Realizing another change was in order, I decided to abandon my doctoral studies and settle on a masters degree in counseling and obtain a license to practice therapy. The next step was to find an environment in which I could balance my need for achievement with my delicate nature.

With little hesitation I jumped at an opportunity to move north outside of the city. Moving from downtown Chicago to the Wisconsin countryside would give me the chance to spend more time in nature—a personal favorite for staying connected to my spirit. The corporate role I took promised to have less intensity than the big city. Perhaps this was the answer I'd been seeking.

Throughout this process I had remained committed to practices that supported the strong connection to my spirit; it was the ONLY way I could manage my sensitivities when they were unpleasantly stimulated by the physical environment, energy around me, or the emotions of others. This commitment made me feel confident as I embarked on this new journey of moving, building a home, and starting my new job. But as fate would have it, the testing of my new skills was about to enter a new phase.

Over the next eight years I would hold five different roles in two different corporate organizations with increasing responsibility. My final destination was a Senior Director role in the financial services industry, and though the intensity level of toxicity and challenge took a jump with each promotion, the proficiency of my spiritual skills kept close pace. I continued to practice regularly at home, and also began integrating them into the workplace. Whether I was interacting with a team member or the CEO, I no longer hid the fact that I lived from a space of spirituality.

My final test of skill and integration was more than I could have anticipated or even imagined. The past focused primarily upon building resiliency when my ego *rather than my spirit* was in the driver's seat. But here I was called to build strength of another sort. The kind that could survive personal attack on my character, my values, and integrity. In a perverse play on politics and circumstances beyond my control, one that only the Universe and my Higher Self could effectively construct, the final crescendo came with termination from my job. This was like nothing I had ever experienced before, and without strong internal guidance and faith as my compass, I certainly would not have weathered the storm so gracefully.

The six months leading up to the fateful day were nothing short of emotionally grueling. The actions of the personalities I was tangling with were guided by ego and fear, and I had no choice but to remain steadfast in connection to my spirit and listen closely to the guidance. A daily practice was to stand in front of my bathroom mirror repeating the affirmation, "I am strong, I am powerful, I am of God." This simple but profound practice reminded me of my connection to something so much larger than myself. It reaffirmed that everything is impermanent and that soon enough the tides would change. It would also help me surrender to the finality of the situation, step out in faith, and purse my dream of, entrepreneurship. In fact, I'd been diligently preparing for independence for nearly a year. I had even created a company name, logo, and business plan. My ego had prevented me from cutting the cord, but now I knew the time had come for me to share a different aspect of myself with the world.

That was four years ago. Today I find myself blessed to be doing work that puts me into a state of joy and alignment with my spirit. My business model has evolved to include all of the activities that energize me while benefiting others, including business and life coaching, spiritual counseling, intuitive readings, teaching workshops, and sharing my message through speaking engagements. Clients seek me out when they are struggling with changes, major life transitions, or restlessness regarding their deeper purpose in life. Together we partner to develop a plan of discovery and action that will take them to their next higher ground. And no surprise, working with Highly Sensitive People is one of my favorite areas of focus. It's here of course, that I'm able to most fully utilize my skills. Having the opportunity to share with others the tools and techniques I've cultivated through life lessons is work that allows me to live from a space of full authenticity as a sensitive, evolve my soul, and feed my spirit … finally.

ABOUT THE AUTHOR: Tiffany's coaching style focuses on the whole person—values, motivations, relationships, and challenges. Her unique background of over 25 years of business experience, training in clinical psychology and practice as an intuitive and medium assist her in melding the worlds of business and spirituality by guiding individuals and organizations to access the brilliance of their whole selves. She has a particular passion around sharing her personal toolkit designed for navigating the world as a Highly Sensitive Person. Tiffany holds an MA in Counseling Psychology from the Adler School of Professional Psychology, a MS in HR from Loyola University Chicago and is a Licensed Professional Counselor.

Tiffany Guske
Sensitivity Expert, Coach, Speaker, & Workshop Facilitator
tiffanyguske.com
tiffany@tiffanyguske.com
facebook.com/yourspiritcoach

The Mother's Day Card
Sandra Filer

I woke up on Mother's Day filled with emptiness. Without my mother it was just another day. I drove to the grocery store on auto-pilot, windshield wipers going back and forth, wiping away the spatter from the rain. Once inside, I blankly stared at my shopping basket filled with cat food, bird seed, and whipped cream, a host of random items, and realized that I had forgotten my wallet. I let out a sigh, and my gaze went to the aisle in front of me. It was the greeting card aisle. That aisle where you'd find the Hallmark cards on display. The cards embellished with carefully crafted words and sentiments, celebrating our mothers. Sprinkled with glitter.

Later, as I sat down to write this, I thought back to the same time last year, when I selected her Mother's Day card, knowing it would be the last. My mother's body had been crippled with ALS. This dis-ease took her ability to swallow, speak, walk, and finally, to write, away. She spent several months trapped inside of her failing frame, surviving on the liquid pumped into her stomach via a feeding tube. It was agonizing to watch her struggle, especially when trying to speak, when all that would escape her lips were inaudible sounds. The only way my mother was able to communicate was with a children's erasable writing board, her gnarled hands struggling to hold the stylus as she scribbled words of reply to our questions, or by nodding or shaking her head. We'd read the message and then ... she'd erase it. Nothing left behind but a memory of the conversations.

Our relationship had been tumultuous over the years. One of my earliest memories is when I was around the age of six, traversing down the stairs in the dark to get a trash bag. I can still hear my mother saying, "Now be a good girl, Sandi. Just get the trash bag. I'm going to stand at the top of these stairs and watch you."

Being the dutiful daughter, not wanting to get in trouble, down the stairs I went, my heart beating wildly. I darted into the kitchen, snatched the bag, and approached the flight of stairs. True to her promise, my mother stood at the top of the stairs.

As my foot touched the first step, she yelled out, "Look out, Sandi, there is someone behind you!"

Terror rose in my chest and I ran up those stairs as fast as my feet would go! To my horror, my mother was doubled over in laughter. When I reached the top, she gasped, "You should have seen your face! And, how fast you ran!"

To this day, I do not like to go downstairs in the dark.

Another event that haunts me took place in the bedroom I shared with my sister. One night, as we prepared for bed, the door flew open and there stood our mother, with a nylon pulled over her face like a burglar. Terrified, my sister and I let out bloodcurdling screams, and Mother once again burst into laughter. To this day, I am hesitant to look inside of closets.

As I grew up, I was also given a host of nicknames, none of which were endearing. When I received attention from my father, I was "Snooky."

"Whatever Snooky wants," she would quip sarcastically, "Snooky gets."

Another nickname, "Queenie," reared its ugly head whenever my grandmother gave me a gift.

The worst, though, was when she referred to me as a "snake."

"You are like a snake in the grass, Sandi, always going behind my back to get what you want."

Snooky. Queenie. A snake in the grass. It was difficult to enjoy anything that was given to me because I felt so guilty for having it.

Time passed, our parents divorced, and life just got more chaotic. Mother married a man she had met in the companion column of the newspaper; he was later murdered in their apartment. Years later, he was followed up with an alcoholic preacher. He drank himself to death. Mother's circumstances continued to deteriorate, and before her passing she was living in a travel trailer parked in my brother's yard.

Why do I share something so personal? As I write, it feels a bit disrespectful, yet I am driven by the need to share our story because it is one of tragedy and compassion. And, I know in my heart that if I can heal the relationship I had with my mother, perhaps you can heal yours too.

This healing began over a decade ago, in a tiny library staffed with two elderly ladies on a small island off the coast of Florida. As my eyes scanned the shelves of books, it suddenly appeared: Louise Hay's "You Can Heal Your Life."

As I picked up the book and began flipping through the pages, I immediately knew it was time to heal my life, including my relationship with my mother. You see, without consciously doing it, I was walking my mother's path. I, too, had repeated a pattern of marrying emotionally unavailable and unfaithful men. Finding this book would be the catalyst to healing those old wounds of the past and start moving in a new direction.

In 2006, with the encouragement of my then-boyfriend, I took the Heal Your Life® Workshop Leader Training, never imagining that this one week of intensive training would ultimately provide me with the necessary experience and understanding to move forward in my Life. This certainly didn't seem to be the case at the beginning, for though I felt ready for the training, the Universe conspired to put this to the test. First, my outgoing flight to sunny and magical Orlando, Florida departed late. When we landed I raced to the hotel, arriving in a frenzy and ready for a cocktail, only to learn the bar was closed. The next insult to injury was that there was no room available for me. Now truly agitated, I began tapping my fingernails on top of the check-in counter. Finally, I was directed to spend the night in the room of one of the co-facilitators of the training. Lugging my baggage over to her room, I was greeted by a less-than-enthusiastic woman clad in a leopard print nightie.

My inner-child was effectively triggered by all of this and I laid myself on the bed and cried myself to sleep. This would be the beginning of the journey within.

Throughout the week, I delved deeply into discovering how the actions of my mother impacted my adult life. Exercise after exercise, Kleenex after Kleenex, the exploration went deeper and from this I was made aware of how to navigate through the old patterns and beliefs to re-create new behaviors to re-design my life, all while accepting the past as it had been. This was instructive, to say the least! One of the most instrumental things I heard Louise say was, "If your parents are still alive and you don't understand something they did, ask them."

Ask them. Something that seems so simple, yet requires so much courage. Just how does one approach a parent and ask such a difficult question? I decided it was worth approaching because I truly wanted to understand Mother's behavior—the actions and words that had left such deep scars on my heart.

Finally, I summoned the nerve to ask her why she had scared me when I was a little girl. I don't actually remember where we were or how it all went down; what I do vividly recall, however, was my mother's response. "To make you stronger," she said, simply and directly, "It was what my father did to me."

Wow, I thought, this actually makes sense. As Louise Hay had also said, "We are all victims of victims."

While this certainly did not justify the behavior, it did give me a window into my mother's perspective, and her own painful past. She was merely operating from what she knew, and in her woundedness, she was repeating the old patterns passed down during her own childhood. Her own insecurities and feelings of unworthiness, being projected out into the lives of those in her sphere of influence. Having this awareness changed everything for me. I was able to better understand her behavior as a person— raised in a home filled with abuse, criticism, and secrets, then charged with playing the role of my mother. And, after really listening with my heart, to gain a deeper understanding on a soul level, the anger that I had held onto for decades melted into compassion. If I had to choose one lesson for which I am eternally grateful, it is how that one simple, yet impactful change helped heal my heart and open up a new dynamic for us! It is one I would later treasure.

So many years, I would stand staring blankly at the Mother's Day cards. Picking one after another up, reading the messages, and saying, "Nope, that's not my mother. None of that is true." I'd finally settle with a generic message simply saying that I loved her. Period.

On August 30, 2017, I stepped outside of the care facility to make a phone call. It was around 8:30 p.m., and I looked up into the Michigan sky, I saw the tiniest of snowflakes falling down. How could this be possible in the summer? Goosebumps went up and down my entire body and I knew deep in my heart that the time for our mother's spirit to leave her body was fast approaching. The call ended and I made my way back to her bedside. My sister was there too, and we each held one of her hands and through our tears spoke our goodbyes. At 9:44 her heart stopped and for a moment, so did ours.

Today, I had no card to buy. Yet, if I did, it would be filled with sentiments of how much I did love her because she taught me so much. Dolores Bette gave me the opportunity to find compassion in my heart and ultimately, forgiveness for being the mother she was and not the mother I thought she should be. She was always doing the best she could and, at the end of the day, that is all any of us can do.

ABOUT THE AUTHOR: Sandra J. Filer, MBA, is an enthusiastic, high energy, believer in the human capacity to achieve whatever the mind can conceive. She specializes in working with ambitious women seeking fulfillment in their life and work. Her approach is heartfelt, effective, and immediately applicable. As the US East Coast Heal Your Life® Teacher & Coach Trainer she delivers life-changing certification programs grounded in the teachings of Louise Hay. Also known as The Happy Goddess®, her ultimate goal is to guide her clients far away from that inner critic and deeply into self-love and appreciation through coaching, retreats, and workshops.

Sandra J Filer
The Happy Goddess®
thehappygoddess.com
diosafeliz@hotmail.com
713-201-2020

From Avoidance to Embrace
Alison Anderson

"You're eating gluten again?!" my client asked incredulously, when she learned that I was indulging in foods that, at one time, I had avoided due to a long-term sensitivity. Her confusion did not surprise me, given that most alternative health practitioners were teaching about the negative consequences of eating allergens such as gluten. After all, I was once one of those experts who enthusiastically preached about the benefits of an elimination diet, which entailed avoiding common allergens and sensitivities. Over time though, my expanding knowledge, awareness, and intuition led me to blaze a courageous new trail with my diet and wellbeing.

When I was little, my parents did an excellent job of keeping sugary and processed substances to a minimum. They put their attention on making home-cooked family dinners at least five times a week and thoughtfully provided my brother and I with balanced lunches for school. My mom sometimes included a loving note in my lunchbox, reinforcing how important meal time and togetherness was for our family.

While I liked sugar, I always gravitated toward vegetables first. I instinctively ate my broccoli before having a chocolate chip cookie. This approach was in vast contrast to my brother, who was six years older and refused to touch anything green on his plate! I was also the child who methodically organized and counted my Halloween candy, consumed it slowly over the next few months and then abidingly, at the request of my mom, threw out any uneaten pieces.

At around the age of ten, I developed a sensitivity to raw apples.

This caused the roof of my mouth to itch ferociously after only a few bites. A few other fruits that had skin, like peaches, also needed to be peeled. Otherwise, my diet remained consistent throughout my childhood. Little did I know then how integral food would become in my journey.

In my twenties, after college, and with my apple sensitivity still intact, I moved to the Big Apple (aka New York City), to start my career in business. It was the age of the dot-coms, which meant that most of my evenings were spent at sponsored Internet parties. During the week, my dinner often consisted of a small plate of fried appetizers and a few cosmopolitans. After living this lively lifestyle for about a year, my body was thrown into a tailspin when I received an alarming message that something was not right. My main symptom, which eventually led me on a quest for answers, was intense and debilitating stomach pain. It prevented me from going to work and, even more disheartening, made me cancel fun social plans with friends.

My mom offered me advice from Adele Davis, an early twentieth century nutrition pioneer, who recommended increasing one's daily fiber intake by eating an apple a day.

"Thanks, Mom. Apples make my tongue itch," I replied.

Despite my reaction, I tried her suggestion, but it was to no avail; my stomach still hurt. I felt lost and alone in this struggle. In due time, I sought out a primary care physician and then a gastroenterologist. Both of their answers were the same: change your diet. I took this recommendation seriously and hired a nutritionist who provided me with a list of foods to include and avoid as part of my daily diet. At work I stocked my cabinet drawer with cardboard tasting rice cakes and a jar of peanut butter (gluten-free products and almond butter were unheard of back then).

As I was reviving my health, I was also watching my dear friend Marci fight her own battle with colon cancer. Marci and I had met during high school, when we were both working at a local chocolate shop. Prior to the health struggles we both experienced in our early twenties, chocolate and sugar were our go-to solution to mend a broken heart, make up for a bad grade, and soothe any stress that might come with the college application process.

During our health challenges, we decided to step away from the chocolate and follow a macrobiotic diet instead. At the time, macrobiotics was a popular way of eating and healing that was supposed to balance a person's yin and yang elements. Although I was inspired by Marci's courageous and time-consuming efforts preparing authentic macrobiotic cuisine at her home in Connecticut, I took the easier route and regularly ventured to a local macrobiotic restaurant in New York City. When Marci passed, I awoke to the fact that one diet, in this case macrobiotics, despite all its healing properties, does not fit or heal all individuals.

At the age of twenty-seven, when I lost my dear friend, I gained a new-found commitment to my own health, and then to sharing this passion with others. Thankfully, my digestive ailment had healed by that time. My belief, at the time, was that physical health was mostly dependent on physical solutions, such as eating the "right" foods and avoiding the "wrong" foods. In my mind, every food either had angel wings and a halo or a sharp pointy tail and devils' ears. This belief was reinforced as I advanced my avid interest in the healing properties of food by getting certified as a health coach and receiving a master's degree in Clinical Nutrition. I joyfully worked with clients and became a sought-after expert in the field, landing a consultancy role giving regular corporate workshops at a Fortune 500 company. My clients trusted my wisdom and expressed their desire to follow my eating regime. They all wanted my secret, thinking that it was the golden ticket to weight loss and longevity.

I was flexible and loving in my approach with clients, yet

internally my relationship to food became a part-time religion. I would regularly cleanse my system with specific foods, shakes, and other concoctions to help support my body's detoxification pathways. I said, "I can't have that" more times than I care to admit. Coming from a place of deprivation was not helpful. In the abstract, I loved the advice I had received from a professional training program, to "focus on adding nourishing foods to the diet like leafy greens, 'super foods,' and ancient grains." However, my mental focus, which I did not fully realize at the time, was on avoidance. Looking back, I recognize how fear and blame based my eating habits had become.

The guidelines I created for my clients felt good to me and were based on clinical experience and research. However, some clients thrived, and some did not. Most who succeeded, did so only temporarily. Giving up all sugar, gluten, dairy, corn, soy, and the like was not easy. My clients came to sessions saying things like, "I cheated..." or "I did okay for a few weeks and then I fell off the wagon." Their self-sabotage kicked in and they reverted to self-blame. I could relate.

Luckily, early in my career, I had been introduced to a healing process based on ancient Chinese medicine. For those clients open to incorporating this Eastern wellness approach during sessions, it helped bring in more self-love and less self-defeating attitudes around food and body image. While this process is more accepted in the mainstream health coaching world today, it was looked upon as "odd" and "fringe" ten years ago. When I first learned this set of techniques, I too thought it was strange and "too good to be true." Still, I could not deny evidence that consistent and sustaining transformations were happening for my clients and myself. My heart was pulled to know and learn more. I delved deep into the study of the brain and the concept that we store beliefs, traumas, and emotions within our cells. Dr. Bruce Lipton's book *The*

Biology of Belief became my new wellness paradigm.

My fascination with the human body and its connection to the emotional and spiritual plane exploded! I became a student of kinesiology (aka muscle testing) and discovered that the power of my health was within me, not outside of myself, like I had once thought. Instead of moving away from myself and my own intuitive knowing, I was turning inward for guidance and answers. I naturally leaned into this new empowered way of being and started changing who I was from the inside out. I awoke to the idea that the subconscious part of my brain drove my behaviors, and essentially my life, at least 90% of the time. I learned how to work with, and become friends with, my subconscious mind to help bring forth a new reality in my body and my life. It was as if the cobwebs inside my being were losing their strength and I could see life through a different lens. My intuition became strong and my connection to myself, Spirit, and life itself expanded.

I soon discovered the power I had to transform not only my subconscious beliefs, but also my allergies and sensitivities. I had some of my biggest "aha" moments exploring the foods and substances that I reacted negatively to. There were quite a few! For instance, when I addressed my long-standing apple allergy, I had to revisit my childhood and understand that this allergy stemmed from a traumatic situation I had faced when I was eating fruit. I then created new beliefs at the subconscious level of my brain that reinforced how I wanted to feel after eating apples and any other fruit with skin on it. Ironically, one of the ways in which I resolved my sensitivity to nuts was by exploring a few relationships that were literally, driving me nuts! Some foods, like gluten, were not simple to incorporate back into my life. However, I followed the energy and my symptoms until there was full resolution. By doing so, I became less rigid, let go of my "I can't" attitude, stopped blaming food for everything, and brought forth more expansion into my world.

In every healing opportunity, I believe there is at least one gift. Shortly after releasing many of my food issues, the love of my life appeared serendipitously. Much to my surprise, my new-found relationship to food led me to meet and marry my amazing husband. Before working with my sensitivities and allergies, I had done a lot of inner work on deserving and calling forth "the one." By adding back into my diet all the foods that I had avoided for years, my search for a sweet and fulfilling life partner surfaced from within me. Also, while I met my husband after I had healed my food phobias, I am confident that he will support me in all life decisions, even if it means changing my diet again to learn more about myself and my body's needs.

It took years of life experience and experimentation to find that, for me, food avoidance was not creating the life I longed for. I wanted to have choice with everything in my life, including food. I chose to stop being a prisoner to my food. Within weeks of meeting my husband, I also took a brave leap with my career by departing from my role as a clinical nutritionist. Today, I empower others by helping to illuminate their path and inner truth. Together, my clients and I uncover and release the energy blocks that are keeping them stuck in health and in life. My client who questioned me about my choice to eat gluten again is now also enjoying it, despite years of severe intolerance.

It is common for a health coach to say, "How you do food is how you do life." Food can indeed be a great mirror, and it certainly was for me. This mirroring concept continues to teach me so much about myself and the relationships around me. As I released my food allergies, I gained the gifts of freedom, love, and understanding that I carry forth in my work, my relationships, and other parts of my life, too.

ABOUT THE AUTHOR: Alison Anderson is the owner of Healthful Direction, a comprehensive wellness company. Alison's highly intuitive and collaborative style helps melt away limiting "roadblocks" around the areas of food allergies, health concerns, life challenges, phobias, and more. She uses high speed mindset change processes to uncover underlying core messages from the body to restore wellbeing. Alison holds a Master of Science in Clinical Nutrition, is a Certified Health Coach, and is professionally trained and self-taught in many energy healing modalities. She has more than twelve years of experience working with clients throughout the world and is passionate about helping them live the best version of themselves—mind, body, and soul.

Alison Anderson, M.S., CHHC
Intuitive Energy Healer
Healthful Direction – Healing from Within
alison@healthfuldirection.com
Complimentary 30 min session: healthfuldirection.com/contact

Mowing My Dirt
Kat Hoyer

That Night

There is a scar on my kitchen floor from that night—the night that I saved my own life. The night that my then-husband and I got into yet another argument over God-knows-what. In a rage of frustration I threw my plate to the floor. It shattered. Spaghetti splattered everywhere. I didn't care. I left it. I left.

I drove out into an unseasonably late-in-the-year snowstorm and ended up on unfamiliar roads. There were sharp curves with steep embankments. I drove away that night to get away from the pain of fighting but the more I drove the more I wanted to get away from the pain of everything; the pain of living. The pain of feeling like a failure as a wife, a friend, an employee, a sister, and a daughter. I wanted to end everything and I began to plan how I could drive off one of the embankments and make it look like an accident. I didn't want to hurt anyone in my life or have them wondering why I did it; in fact, I wanted to protect them. I wanted to free them of the burden I believed I placed on their shoulders. Then one person popped into my mind, one little person. My son. He was too young to understand and I knew I didn't want him to grow up without a mommy. These thoughts—these suicidal ideations—weren't new. They had been plaguing me for several months and were becoming more and more frequent and were feeling more and more substantiated.

Suddenly, in what I know now was a Divine Intervention, a song came on the radio. I was listening to a station I never listened to and the song was one I hadn't heard in years. It was a song that played at the funeral of a high school acquaintance that had taken his own life by driving into the path of a semi-truck. The song jolted me back to reality and suddenly I was no longer planning how to die, I was planning to live. When I returned home, my son and his dad were playing a board game and the kitchen was cleaned up. To this day we've never spoken of that night, and he still doesn't know the hell my mind was putting me through.

The next morning I reached out for counselling. I knew I didn't want to die but I had no idea how to live. I spent the better part of a year in therapy with an amazing therapist who helped me along as much of my journey as I was able to manage at that point. It took me several sessions to even tell her the story of that night and of my suicidal thoughts and plans but when I finally did, we were able to get to work. I got stronger. I began seeing that life was worth fighting for but I had no idea how much more I would learn about myself over the next five years. I had no idea this was just the beginning.

The Fight in my Mind

The stronger I got, the more distant my husband got. As I began to attempt to love myself again I could sense that his love was displaced. Not gone, just not with me any longer. In true women's intuition form, he said her name one morning and I knew. I just knew. I began to replace the fight for my life with the fight for my marriage. I pulled out all the stops with date nights and attempts at intimacy. I tried harder to be more domestic, funnier, anything I thought might win him back. I tried to rally others on my behalf; friends, family, coworkers. Until one day I realized I was fighting to win. I was not fighting for my marriage but to win against her. It was then that I threw in the towel and thought I had changed my focus. And in some ways I had. Though I wasn't trying to win him back anymore, there was still a fight going on—a fight in my mind.

I had taken inventory of every single bad thing that had ever been said to me and I would play it on repeat in my mind, sometimes consciously, but mostly subconsciously. I kept a running tab of every mistake I had ever made and clung to those mistakes as proof of why I was a bad person or why I was undeserving of love or a good job or friends. These thoughts became my truth. These thoughts were slowly chiseling away at everything I thought I was and everything I hoped I would be. I was mostly unaware this fight was going on in my mind, I just knew I was manifesting one challenging experience after another. I told a good friend one day through sobbing tears, "I want to pick myself up but I can't find my bootstraps!"

The Downward Spiral

My life felt like a downward spiral. Have you ever dropped a coin into one of those funnels? You know the one that starts out really big at the top, then seems to move very slowly toward the bottom until it reaches the tubular part of the funnel? Then the spin picks up and begins to move so fast it actually loses the graceful rotation it originally had on the way down. The coin gyrates and thrashes until it crashes through the tunnel. That was me for the next three years.

A few months after the divorce was filed, I lost my dream job. I was downsized with about thirty other people because the company was losing money hand over fist. But that didn't stop me from replaying every single misstep on the job on a loop in my mind of how I could have potentially caused it and/or prevented it.

It didn't help that the very next job I landed was in the middle of its own downward spiral. The person that hired me was let go two weeks after I started and one by one, everyone I knew in the organization was gone within a few months. This was an organization that I had a great deal of respect for and partnered closely with over the course of several years prior. I had become personal and professional friends with many of the people that worked there. As they left, I felt alone and confused and it showed in my performance. My tenure there was less than six months and every single day felt like the spinniest, most out of control part of the coin funnel.

I then found what would ultimately become the third job in as many years that I would lose. I thought my luck had changed but I realized I was just the coin at the top of the funnel—gracefully, rhythmically, and slowly spiraling down. It was more than just the fact that the company wasn't in alignment with my morals and values. It was that, yet again, I couldn't gain control of my inner dialogue.

The Breaking Point

I had always been an outwardly happy and positive person and I believe it's who I am, who most of us are, as a default. So even during these times of what I've referred to as a functional depression over the course of these three years, it was hard for me to pinpoint not only the cause of these negative feelings but more importantly that I was even having them. It just felt like a funk. I finally realized while journaling, that there were things I was saying to myself that I wouldn't say to my worst enemy. And I certainly wouldn't allow another human to speak to me the way I was speaking to myself.

This discovery was so very eye-opening, yet I didn't know how to break the cycle. Affirmations felt silly and fake. And my thoughts had become my new belief system.

The Shift

I would love to say there was one colossal shift that changed everything but the truth is the shift was comprised of thousands of tiny pivots. But the one monumental pivot was the day I was mowing my dirt. You see, my front lawn was very sparse, yet it still needed to be mowed. Think of a bald man with a few hairs. He still needs to get haircuts, right? So when I mowed my sparse lawn, dirt would fly everywhere. I would have it in my hair, my clothes, even up my nose by the time I was done. And to make matters worse, my lawn had a slope just steep enough that I really struggled to push the mower up and would have to run to keep up with the mower when going down. I'm sure I was a sight to see.

While mowing my dirt, fighting tears and thinking how much I hated my ex for my current situation and hated my job because I didn't make enough money to pay someone to mow my lawn, it hit me that I didn't want to feel like this anymore. I was sick and tired of feeling sorry for myself, of hating myself, and of no longer being the happy person I knew I was meant to be. So in that moment, in front of the white picket fence lined with red and yellow tulips with dirt flying everywhere, I decided to make a mental list of the things I was grateful for. I'd heard about gratitude from Oprah and even tried and failed a few times to keep gratitude journals but I didn't really understand why gratitude worked until that moment. My list began with the fact I had a lawn, then that I had a mower to mow it with, and a garage to keep it in, and strength in my body to push the mower. As I began to think these new thoughts, something in me shifted. I felt different. My thoughts were changing my emotions! I continued to make mental lists of everything in my life that I had to be grateful for. Before I knew it, my dirt had been mowed and I was loving life.

Now I would love to tell you that I love mowing my lawn now, but the truth is, I pay someone to do it. But what I can tell you is that I realized my thoughts were keeping me stuck, and that was incredible news. Because that meant that if my thoughts were the only thing keeping me where I was, feeling sad, angry, and hurt; my thoughts could also take me where I needed to go, feeling motivated, inspired, and grateful to be alive. Upon this discovery an entire world of people, podcasts, videos, and books poured into my life. I had used that shift to literally *change my mind!*

Today, I know better than to believe everything I think. I am able to recognize negative thought patterns quickly and shift them accordingly. I've been given the gift of teaching others how to do this on a daily basis in a way that empowers them to truly be the driver of their own success.

ABOUT THE AUTHOR: Kat Hoyer is the creator of STEER Your Life Coaching® and founder of SYLC Consulting. After a series of unexpected detours in her life Kat was determined to step into the driver's seat again and learn from these experiences in a way that could help others, and she created the proprietary process known as STEER. Kat has also developed SYLC Certification curriculum for other coaches and leaders that allows them to utilize this proprietary process with their own clients and teams. SYLC Consulting is currently headquartered in Akron, Ohio, with associates in Miami and San Antonio.

Kat Hoyer, CEO, SYLC Consulting
860-792-6224 (o) 330-256-7081 (c)
kat@sylcconsulting.com
KatHoyer.com
Akron, OH / Angola, IN

The Call
Brenda Colter

The day my father died was the first day of the rest of my life. If you're anything like me, there are certain inevitable events in your life that have not yet taken place, but for which you have already envisioned your reaction. Growing up, I had convinced myself that when my father passed I would not give a damn. I figured I would get a call from my Auntie Benita, just as she had called when my great-uncle and Grandmommie died. In fact, aside from Facebook exchanges, deaths were the only time I ever heard from my father's side of the family. Benita would tell me he was gone and I'd continue on without a single misstep. Still, my hand shook visibly when I looked down at my ringing cell phone that day and saw Auntie Benita's name. I knew before I answered that something was wrong. Someone was dead. I could hear my heart beating in my ears as I answered.

"Hello?" It came out as a question to which I really didn't want an answer.

"Brenda?" she said, then continued without awaiting a response, "Your dad ... he passed away ..."

My mouth instantly went completely dry, as if I had attempted to make a snack out of a handful of cotton balls. My fingers went numb and I had a very difficult time holding the phone. I kept flexing them to get the blood moving and even cracked my knuckles a few times, hoping to regain some feeling. I asked some questions; she gave some answers, none of which I can recollect. I remember feeling as though someone had drained all the blood from my body. The room got cold and began to spin and I was spinning with it. I was dizzy and felt completely empty. It would be days before I would revisit this moment in an attempt to unpack my reaction. In that moment, all I knew were feelings of desolation and confusion. As I stood there, listening to the sound of my wildly beating heart, I remember thinking that my father's heart would never beat again.

The Arrival

I don't remember the drive to the home my father had shared with my stepmother, Charlotte, a home in which I had always felt like an intruder. I don't remember why I felt like I had to get there *right then*. All I knew was, I couldn't wait. I couldn't breathe. I couldn't think. I couldn't feel. I do remember wondering why I felt such a sense of urgency. Then I wondered why I felt that I shouldn't feel a sense of urgency. Nothing made sense. Confusion kept my head foggy and before I knew it, I was sitting outside their home and Auntie Benita was tapping on my window. I got out of my car and like a prisoner walking to execution, I slowly trudged behind her into the house.

The longer I remained inside, the emptier I felt. Sitting there in that room with the paternal side of my family, I realized that though we shared the same blood, we omitted very different energy. They clearly experienced a closeness to this situation I didn't possess. That's what my father's death had become—a "situation." Then more people began to arrive, people of no blood relation but who seemed even more upset than I—at least, more upset than I appeared to be. No one knew I was dying inside; *I* didn't even know, for I had convinced myself I wasn't allowed. *How dare you feel right now?* I demanded, *You, who only called him when you needed clarification on a Bible verse or study lesson.* So I sat and presented a mask to the group. It was an austere demeanor I'd exhibited plenty of times in my life and which had always proven to be one of my most valuable defense mechanisms.

Now, however, it didn't feel as valuable. I just sat with an awkward half-smile plastered on my face. Every now and again someone would whisper, "Who is that?" accompanied by subtle points and head nods in my direction. These were followed by confused-sounding responses of "Oooooooohhhhh, his oldest?" or "I thought Antwan was the oldest…" Then there was the gracious gentlemen who upon learning of my relation to my father exclaimed, "I didn't even know you existed!" It was this man, and his pitying gaze, that made my eyes, finally, well up with tears.

No wonder no one knows about me. I'm not here. I'm invisible. I've always been invisible. I don't belong here. I glanced around the living room at the family photos. More awful thoughts began to hit me. *This is the home of a family with three sons. Nothing to acknowledge the daughter/adversary that has been all but absent for years.*

I attempted to replace my self-pity with grief, but that didn't work. Grief is an emotion that overtakes a person. It can't be summoned or mustered. These people were mourning a son, a brother, a husband, a father, a mentor, a teacher, a friend. What would I miss? Who was I mourning?

The Epiphany

Five days later, I got a text from Charlotte, asking if I wanted to speak at the funeral. My response was simple: "Yes ma'am, I can do that."

And then I panicked and called my mother.

"I don't really know him," I whined. "What do you say about a person who didn't even like you?"

My mother half-coddled, half-chastised me with the same speech she'd used for years: "Your father loves you. He has always loved you. You don't know his story and you both are equally as stubborn. You both played a part in making that relationship what it was or wasn't, but he has never NOT loved you."

I was still anxious when I hung up the phone, but something told me I needed to see this thing through to the end. So I spent a few days reviewing the sporadic conversations my father and I had and perusing the piles of Bible verses and studies he had sent me. His notes were painstakingly articulated to ensure that I, a layperson, could grasp the crux of what he was attempting to explain.

It happened most unexpectedly. I was lying in bed, reading the communication between my father and myself after my oldest son was shot during a robbery. Suddenly, I realized that my father had been coaching me, mentoring me, counseling me all along. I began to flip through all of our communication at hyper speed. As I did, I realized that I stopped being able to see through my tears pages ago. The paper was wet and the tears that filled my eyes had spilled over onto the pages in my hand. I was on the floor trying to catch my breath. Could it be? Is this real? Was it possible that the man that I long considered my adversary had been operating as my ally all this time? My chest ached as it heaved spastically. I couldn't seem to take in enough air! I clawed at my chest. I had had enough panic attacks in the past to know what it was, but this was different. This was the big one. I was going to die. No one would ever know what I had realized. All of my father's work would be for naught. Now I felt it, all the emotions that had been missing when I got the call: pain, loss, abandonment. I was mourning my father, and it hurt so good.

The Farewell

One of my three brothers holds me steady as we walk onto the stage. We all have things to say. Different things. Important things. We all had different relationships with our father. I listen as my brothers painstakingly say their farewells to the man who molded them into the men they are today. They're so regal, I can't help but to admire them. I'm proud to be their sister. Now it's my turn. I step to the podium and find my mother in the crowd. She gives an almost imperceptible nod, and so I begin:

When I was a little girl, I thought our father was magic. It's funny the things that we remember when tragedy strikes. When I received news of his passing, I rushed to his home and in the car, I got flashes of his days as my own personal magician. See, we spent a lot of time in the car together during my early years traveling to and from my grandmommie's home in Cleveland Ohio. Well, it felt like forever back then. I remember, he would play music and sing, and this was when the magic would happen, because he would remove his hands from the wheel and drive with his knee and just clap away all while smiling at me and I would marvel. I would think 'Wow! That's amazing!" I still can't do that even now ... He was my daddy, and I believed he was magic.

As most of you know, our father was a man of few words. He was one of the few people left in this world who spoke in actions. Whether it be a smile as bright as the sun, or a scathing glance of reprimand, he made his point clear. But it was this very gift that made his words so powerful. For when he did speak, we knew that it would be something worth saying, hence worth listening to. From gracing the halls of South High School as DJ TC Tetronite, or blessing a congregation with his immeasurable ability to explicate the Word of God, he ... touched ... lives. Even over five hundred miles apart, I could text him ONE question about the bible and within days I would have a delivery of chapters, verses, and notes to help me better understand whatever was causing my confusion. He was our dad, and we believed he was magic.

So today, we get to thank him. We get to honor him. We get to thank God for him. We as the people whose lives he has touched get to be the manifestation of his prayers. We can take his lessons and his teachings and show him that the wisdom, growth, and strength that he instilled in us actually took hold. And as we are

*discussing this husband, this son, this brother, this uncle, this
mentor, this teacher, this pastor ... I just want everyone to know
that he is our father, and he is magic.*

The "Blesson"

A dear friend of mine once told me that some of the toughest
lessons we learn in life can ultimately be blessings; hence the term
"blesson." When I walked off that stage, I felt lighter, more
confident, wiser, and more spiritually enlightened than ever
before. You see, in that moment, when I was writhing in agony on
my bedroom floor, I was indeed dying, but I was also being reborn.
I was blessed to instantaneously receive and absorb all the lessons
my father had bestowed upon me over the years. They played like
a movie reel in my mind, and I could see, hear, and feel our
interactions, not through the eyes of his scorned daughter, but in
the eyes of God's restored daughter. It was in that moment I
realized, I am the answer to my father's prayers. I am the
manifestation of his dreams. And it is my responsibility to be sure
that his legacy lives on.

From that day forward, I realized that all of my steps are indeed
ordered by the Word of God. Not only has this little damaged girl
been restored, but restored to the coach and mentor I am today,
helping women and young girls change the negative thought
patterns that keep them mired in the mud of life. I help them
combine scripture with practical thought awareness strategies to
ensure successful application of life's lessons. Most importantly, I
have been able to take not only the relationship with my father, but
his lessons in spirituality to the next level. In the words of the late,
great Tupac Shakur: "I'm not saying I'm gonna change the world,
but I guarantee that I will spark the brain that will change the
world."

ABOUT THE AUTHOR: Brenda Colter is the owner of HER Beautiful Mind, founder of BeTheReason, and Vice President of SYLC Consulting. Brenda overcame the mistakes of her youth to climb the corporate ladder of a Fortune 500 company before deciding to follow God's calling for her life. Today, she merges her role as life coach/mentor with the Word of God to present it in a way that makes it clear and practical to others. Brenda's mission is to show the world that no matter where you've come from, no matter how you've been burned, it's always possible to rise up from the ashes and begin anew.

Brenda Colter
HER Beautiful Mind
sylcconsulting.com
brendacolter.com
910-633-0102

Embrace the Process

My Journey, Finding my Heart and Soul

Ruthe Hanson Plaché

It has taken a lot of life experience to grasp the meaning of conscious, soulful, spirit-led, and heartfelt living. The journey of finding meaning and living my reality developed over time and through choices, abuses, illnesses, and acceptance, and the deeper meaning is far different than the empty words present at the start. Perhaps it was the emptiness of those words that, in part, inspired me to look for that deeper meaning, until it became imperative for me to live honestly and authentically with myself and others in order to find freedom, joy, and happiness on every level. No more play acting. No more affectation or editing myself or my behaviors.

Thankfully, divine spirit longed to link inseparably with my human spirit. This innate desire for connection and belonging was perhaps my greatest need. Once my human spirit joined with the divine a wonderful thing happened: it was my Divine Nature Activated (DNA). This was the pursuit. I share a few experiences here.

The words "heart" and "soul" were used widely and often in the religious environment into which I was born, grew up, was educated, and into which I married. These words were no doubt the most influential part of any philosophical thought in my life. It wasn't surprising, given that my father was a preacher. The environment was all about words and they were tossed about in every kind of situation. At the end of the service each week there was an invitation to surrender one's heart and soul or rededicate heart and life to spiritual service. It was the guarantee my soul would be saved.

Yes, there were souls to save. Workers in "the field" and missionaries from abroad returned to tell the story of "souls being saved." That was the rhetoric, and though these words became commonplace and ordinary, a seed had been planted in the fertile soil of my curious mind. My grasp of the meaning and impact of these words came later, after a lengthy germination process. My parents were devoted, and focused on their religious beliefs as the cornerstone of our lives. They always wanted to be right and good role models. Their life was all about "doing the work and having a good work ethic." That kind of discipline was great in that it creates resolve, purpose, drive, and resourcefulness. For that, I thank them.

For sure, I have demonstrated some characteristics of an extrovert. I usually jump in the middle of whatever is going on in order to be a part of it. I'm all in from the start. I tend to be proactive and engaged once I know the expectation or plan. This defines my personality in just about anything. My mother shared I was active in her womb and after birth the difference between me and my older brother gave her concern. She said she didn't know what to do with me. I never met a stranger, and I didn't want to take naps or go to bed. Typically she would let me fall asleep playing or investigating something and after I'd fallen asleep on the floor she or my dad would tuck me in. Her description of me was a "busy little girl always wanting something to do or wanting to be in the middle of things." As a result she would find things for me to do, lest I get into trouble.

I love to help. Washing dishes was the greatest fun as early as age two. I loved standing on a chair playing in the water. I still love playing in water and doing dishes. My work in Cosmetology added to this joy by allowing me to wash and style hair. I also loved helping my dad with his vegetable or flower garden. There is a picture of me at a very young age trying to use a long-handled rack although it was impossible. When I was a bit older and we were working side by side he said to me, "Gardeners are born, they're not made." I was delighted, and my love of gardening continues to this day. My plants are like children, they need to be fed, taken care of, and nurtured. I have a fascination with all creative things. Household and outdoor chores are creative projects for me. I love seeing results. It makes me feel good. It's the most important part of my being alive. At age five I wanted to learn to iron. Mother let me start with handkerchiefs, and not knowing how to handle the hot appliance, I promptly ironed my wrist, got a severe burn and the scar is visible to this day. This experience did not dampen my enthusiasm for ironing; in fact, I still love it.

One of the most gratifying experiences with ironing was when I was twelve and we were returning home on a ship from the mission field in the Philippine Islands. I was feeling bored and one day asked the chief engineer if there was something I could do.

"Tell you what," he said, "you can iron my shirts and trousers for twenty-five cents each."

I was ecstatic, and after getting permission from my mother I immediately got to work. I just loved connecting with people where they are and assisting in making their lives better.

As a young woman I attended a four-year Christian college and prepared myself for ministry. I later married a minister, not knowing he would make choices that drew me away from my creative soul and into a system of laws and expectations that separated me from myself and family. I lost my free, open spirit. I became rigid in order to adhere to external demands. I didn't like feeling that way and I didn't like what I saw in the faces of others in that religious community. I had always been a curious soul, energetic and full of life. I remember telling my then-husband (we are no longer together) I was concerned that the church didn't talk about feelings. They made light of anyone who wanted to lead from the heart. It was all about the mind, what we understand or can prove that makes life work. I disagreed. He had a tough time trying to convince me that I could ignore my senses. It seemed being sensitive was the best way for me to be in touch with what really mattered.

In spite of constraints I found ways to grow and create. I loved to cook, to entertain, set a beautiful table with fresh flowers, candles, or greenery. I also found self-expression through singing. I had always loved to sing, studied all through school and college and later obtained a B.A. in Music. Now it became my salvation. I began to be aware the things that made me happy were the very things my soul came to this planet to do. I had a divine right to exercise my heart and passion. I had been doing the best I could under all circumstances but now was beginning to see I was allowing myself to exercise gifts of grace. I knew all good and perfect gifts come from the Creator of all that is, however, I had failed to see my part was to respond to the desires and gifts within, by living them.

I know I came to this planet with a distinct need to connect and work with people. I need to identify with others, see them and seek to appreciate their life experience. That's what I do. I dedicated much of my career to working within the senior community. This was no doubt where I learned the most about patience, respecting, accepting, and admiring others for who they are. Science agrees that the aging adult is most effected by sensory perceptions and in this is normalcy.

Perhaps the most significant life experience that taught me spiritual consciousness and compassionate living was the choice to have children. I was given four, and with each one my heart grew, filling me with a love I never knew was possible. I made two decisions about them. One was to let natural child birth happen—no medications during pregnancy or during the birthing process. Two were born in a clinic and two at home. Those moments were some of the most fulfilling in my life. I was committed to trusting the creative flow from start to finish. The other decision was I would maintain a relationship with all of them, all of my life, no matter what. Making that decision I was able to exercise unconditional love for myself and give them space to find their way. Accepting each of them as special souls and allowing them to be unique beings enriched my own life in conscious awareness. I was blessed with knowing these souls needed me as part of their life and I determined to be true to that trust. We were soul mates; souls orbiting in this vast universe full of heart and process.

In recent months I have been going through a painful and humiliating illness from a serious skin infection. It isn't clear how it started but it has radically transformed my life. I haven't been able to work and have had difficulty with the simplest chores of daily living. This experience has set me on a path of self-discovery like nothing else before it. I have found genuine authenticity is fully lived with vulnerability. Surrendering to all elements in my life allowed my body freedom from the emotional self I had been dealing with for a long time. I didn't realize I was still trying to prove something all the time. It was natural to do nice things or reach out for approval. I was a good mimic. I played along. Anything outside that would have been suspect, ridiculed, and unacceptable. I didn't want to be the recipient of shame. So I played the game. I didn't realize I was compromising myself and my integrity.

I had learned over the years to look inside myself and do reality checks all the way along. I took time to respect my thinking, feelings, and desires. However, it took one life experience after another to finally bring me to the place where I could be completely honest about how I feel, what I am doing, how relationships are affecting my self-worth, where I am working, and whether it is supporting my life in a positive way. One thing I know: unless I'm feeling freedom and am filled up by the experience it's not worth doing.

Life was always full of choices. Being true to myself was the biggest choice of all. It was natural and easy to live a life after someone else's style, expectation, or example. However, as an individual in a very complex and competitive world it took time and inner work to get to what was real for me. The most direct question I continually ask myself is, "Am I being honest about my feelings and senses?" If I am, then I know I am in touch with the deepest part of me—my divine nature lived in this flesh—with all my heart and soul. That, and only that, has led me to a humility that continues to support the unfolding of a process, namely, living in conscious awareness that the simplest form of creation is sacred.

Sharing this process with you has also given meaning to my journey. While what I've learned on this road of discovery is valuable on its own, choosing to pass along experiences has proven more powerful than I could ever have dreamed. This process has opened me to a deeper respect for my truth and essence. It has allowed me to watch in awe as this chapter of my journey is transferred from within myself to you as the reader. It truly is more blessed to give than receive.

ABOUT THE AUTHOR: Ruthe Hanson Plaché is creative and unique in her varied interests and abilities. She is an artist who loves gardening, a certified Life Coach, ordained Minister, BA in Music, Singer, certificated in RCFE Administration/Senior Living, and licensed in Cosmetology. Her life work grants individuality, mutual respect, and unconditional love. Her love for people and their diversity led her to host more than one hundred international students. The beauty industry has supported her dedication to allowing each person's need for acceptance through self-expression and personal identity. However, it is the value of authenticity as a mother of four and "nana" to four that is her priority.

Ruthe Hanson Plaché
Ruthe.me
ruthe36@yahoo.com
Facebook: Ruth E Plache
619-208-4379

The Never-Ending Love Story
Sharon Plaché

As I sat quietly by the lake and watched the sun go down after an amazing week of ThetaHealing® Instructor trainings in Montana, I felt the breeze on my skin, the lingering warmth of the sun, and a sense of deep peace that nature seems to give me. It has been wonderful to listen to the sounds of silence mixed with the purity of birdcalls and whispering leaves. The light dappling on Flathead Lake reminds me of the beauty in life that exists everywhere, every day. These sensations prompt me to remember and recognize the gifts life offers me from its infinite, radiant, vibrant self in every moment.

A lot of my life has been lived with the busyness of the city: business tasks, work, community service, and family obligations. Stepping away from these into a rustic and simple pace of life brings me to a place of deeper meaning in the depths of my heart and soul. This reminds me why I love many of Mother Teresa's quotes, and that one in particular is very special to me:

We need to find God and it cannot be found in noise and restlessness.
God is the friend of silence.
See how in nature - trees, flowers and grass grow in silence;
see the stars, the moon and the sun, how they move in silence ...
We need silence to be able to touch souls.
~ Mother Teresa

Over the past twenty years I have been pursuing a path of greater self-love and curiosity of what else might be possible for myself and my soul's purpose for this life. I have come to realize that in many ways I am a quiet soul.

I thrive with silence and found I need it to survive. Being in the present moment of stillness and possibility is definitely where my heart sings and my soul is refreshed.

This pursuit of self-awareness has led me on a path of greater self-discovery as I seek out wise sources of life and its meaning. ThetaHealing® has been one part of this journey. I was not even looking for this specific kind of insight, so it was much to my surprise that I discovered the very word Theta in the Greek language actually means soul. It is a pathway for soul development and growth. This discovery provided another step for me to realize a greater love for myself and life.

When I asked myself what would I share in this chapter about heart and soul living, I needed to break it down a bit. What do these words mean to me? How do I live with an inner knowing they are the very reason I was created, and are intended to be a reflection of my being here now, present on this planet?

First, the soul—it is the essence of me, the conscious of me; presenting a journey, a process or story of itself from the past, in the present and open-ended possibility for the future. Therefore I see evolution, revelation, and transformation before me.

Second, the heart—this is the source; the pulse sustaining all life forms with its steady rhythm and strength. For life to exist the heart of the matter is this, as long as there is the sustained energetic flow, the beat goes on and all things flourish.

I continued to ask myself, what is this never-ending love story of my inner being, this relationship between heart and soul? How do they work together? Do I need to do something with it? What do I do with the experience? What happens when they just *are* and I let them be?

I was curious, do I need to research or analyze what this living dynamic means? Or is my experience possibly a progression over time and space that is part discovery of myself and the beauty in life which exists all around me?

As a result I am discovering and experiencing, as I am present as the observer of life and myself. The vibrations of my heart and soul are everywhere. They are with me, guiding me on this journey. In fact, they show up in my life as I take next steps everyday, everywhere.

Now, as I reflect on my life, the only times I have felt disconnected from my heart and soul were when I felt obligated to do what someone else told me to do because of their opinion or some binding requirement. I became aware I was trying to live by all the "shoulds" in life, rather than listening to my own inner voice. I was following a construct of someone else's creation, rather than my own. I failed to listen to the pulse and rhythm of my own resident inner being. I was left feeling confused and inadequate.

Over time I have come to realize that taking time to find solace in quietness and confidence, there is a freedom from the busy, noisy barrage of life. This place has allowed me to go into a deeper, inner silence and hear my true voice. I listen for wisdom within, mysteriously knowing I am part of the beat of all life and creation.

Another interesting piece I have observed is the feeling required to give my heart and soul away to someone or something, as though I had divested myself of it and it was no longer mine. However, what if in giving and receiving there actually exists an expression of love and life, heart and soul? How can I give away that which is and always will be a part of my personal identity? I found the more I shared myself *with* myself and with others, there was an infinite reservoir of creative energy and possibility.

Then why do I get upset or tired when I give something away, implying I am now missing it? How can I miss that which is and always will be the infinite well-spring of life?

I realized that I had old limited beliefs about resources of time, energy, money, health, and possibility. As I reviewed family history and then looked at the human experience at large, it seemed everyone was constantly managing or pursuing having enough to resource their survival. This could imply there was barely, not quite, or never enough.

I asked myself, is this really true? What would happen if I started looking through the lens of having plenty or more than enough? Could it be everything I need is available to me in the moment I need it or want it? Possibly, if I truly live in the truth of my heart and soul, life is always flowing, expanding, and providing all the time. Life itself is giving by nature.

After taking a training with Dr. Emoto, back in 2006, I became aware of his reference in the book, "Messages from Water." He talks about the water molecule H_2O, being two parts Hydrogen to one part Oxygen. He explained that the Oxygen was the active part of the molecule and Hydrogen was the receptive/passive part.

He shared the importance of sleep, quiet, and meditation as receptive parts. His suggestion for living in harmony and peace with heart and soul was to cultivate quiet receivers. I will be shown what actions to take from quietly receiving direction. I needed this. Needless to say, the wisdom of this rang true for me and has become a guide and cornerstone of support.

Contemplative thought and its meaning are only available to me as I listen in silence.

Is there value in a state of being? Is it equal to doing?

What happens when I am present with that which sustains all life, the heart, my heart?

What is its message for me, to me?

What happens when I am present with my soul essence, the current state of my consciousness? What gifts does it share in being and becoming?

Is it possible to get away from this never-ending love story whether I see it, acknowledge it, believe it, honor it, feel it, or even listen to it? No, it is always present.

What do I gain when I pretend to disconnect?

What do I experience when I am present with what is?

When I practice self-observation, who is doing the observing and what is being learned?

As a means to finding an inner compass to heart and soul in order to redirect the endless chatter of external dictates, I decided to live alone and give myself space and time to be wholly with myself. I did this for five years after completing on a marriage and all the obligations family and society were expecting of me.

There was a moment when I heard Randy Crawford's song *"Silence"* and knew it was a truth for me –

"Got my mind in the clouds and I want to feel cozy all alone.
Feel the sounds in my ear, I suppose I am a quiet soul.
People say there is no way to escape the loudness in a room.
Wonder how they can live with the noise. I am sure they are fools.

"Listen. While I dispose of it all. I am living in silence.
Listening to vibrating chimes while I enjoy my quiet time in silence.
In Silence.
Yes it is true there are sounds that I love as
they wander through my ears.
Such as waves rolling in and the trees telling stories to the wind.
Silence is a hibernation . . . while all else seems to decay.
A place for me to persuade . . . the noise to fade away.

Listen. While I dispose of it all . . . I am living in silence.
Listening to vibrating chimes while I enjoy my quiet time in silence.
In Silence."

~Randy Crawford

To me, silence represents the white space in design. The part left empty, not filled in. This open space enhances, gives meaning and purpose to that which is filled in, while leaving room and possibility for what is yet to be presented, discovered, or expressed.

To live my life, filled with intention and purposeful creation, I have found silence gives me the sense of being open to no specific thing, yet open to everything. This allows my heart and soul the breath of life they need to share their vision. Allowing the process in delivering a greater awareness of being, which can grow into becoming all they can be, in me as me.

I celebrate and honor all that is known and is coming into being, in the silent, white, receptive space of all possibility. The never-ending love story of life, the union of my heart and my soul functioning freely in tandem with all creation.

To the winds, the waters, the beauty of nature, the majesty of all creation.

"Open for Love to Surprise Me" ... one of my favorite
mantras.
Thank you Life. Thank you Love.
Namaste.

ABOUT THE AUTHOR: Sharon Plaché is a creative and caring intuitive teacher, mentor, and healer. She has been in the Healing Arts since 1989. She is a practitioner, mentor, and teacher of ThetaHealing®, NLP, MER® and Innerwise®. Her retreat center in San Diego offers classes, trainings, aquatic bodywork, therapeutic massage, yoga, meditation, and more. She is grateful to be a practitioner for the Wave Academy, which offers support to Veterans with PTSD. She is passionate about empowering clients to discover, grow, and create in all areas of their lives. Her combined thirty-five years of education and varied life experience gives her compassion and commitment.

Sharon Karise Plaché
SharonPlache.com
info@sharonplache.com
facebook.com/SharonPlache1
619-339-8177

When the Darkness Subsides

Karen Blanchard

I will never forget the screams, the sobbing, of my teenage son. He was draped over my shoulders because he couldn't hold himself up. The words—*Car accident. She's gone.*—ripping us from our lives and transporting us to some hellish dimension.

It's so dark, this place. The emotional pain is so intense every cell in my body feels like it's going to explode. If only someone could take the pain from me, or even if I could get the pain to subside just a little … For two full days I thought my body was going to give away and I was going to die. Before losing my seventeen-year-old daughter, I never would have imagined someone could actually live through that much emotional pain.

At the end of the celebration of life we put a rose on her coffin as it was put into the back of the hearse. The intense sadness was so strong I felt like I was going to go down, but suddenly I had the sensation of being held up by the elbows. It was as though angels had come from heaven to support me in my darkest moment. At this time, I understood the "Footprints" poem, where God carries you in times of difficulty.

That was just the beginning of my grieving process. That process is not linear. At any given moment, a rush of emotions I didn't even think I had—anger, sadness, depression, more anger, fear, guilt, and disbelief—would hit me. It was as if I'd been dumped in a pinball machine, being thrown every which way.

I didn't know what to expect through all of this, or how was I to help my six other children when I was such a mess myself. All I knew was that I couldn't do this alone. I made appointments with counselors and doctors for myself and for my kids. I wanted to make sure they got the emotional care they needed and that, in my pain, I could not give them.

When I didn't think things could any more painful, they did. It was one month after Bethany died; the Christmas holiday was over and the kids were back at school. A new year was beginning, and for me, a new hell. It was so dark, even the sunniest day seemed black. I started taking little naps throughout the day so I didn't have to deal with the night terrors. I cried and sobbed so hard I thought my neighbors could hear me. I couldn't focus; I felt sick all the time, my body was in such agony from the emotional pain; I was dizzy from the medication my doctor gave me; I couldn't go to the grocery store because I would have anxiety/panic attacks; I had irrational fears, such as when my son was sick with a virus and I went into a panic, thinking he would die too, I would wear sunglasses when I went outside, day or night, because when you cry in minus twenty-degree weather your eyes do freeze shut.

I wanted the pain to stop. I participated in destructive behaviors to make me feel better, such as online shopping and drinking excessive amounts of alcohol. I was drunk for three days; I didn't want to feel any more pain. I didn't want my son to hear me sobbing any more. I didn't want to miss my daughter. Three days doesn't seem like a long time considering what I was going through, but it could have developed into a long-term problem. And, all those emotions that I didn't want to feel, on the fourth day when I wasn't drinking they came in like a tidal wave and I felt like I was going to drown. So I learned that you can't ignore, go around, go over, go under or stop at the door of grieving, you need to go through it, one baby step at a time.

As I mentioned earlier there were two days when I literally felt like I was going to die. I thought my body was going to give up from the emotional pain and the physical pain. I've heard of people dying from a broken heart, like when two people have been married for a long time and one of the spouses dies; it doesn't take too long before the other one dies too. I always thought there was a sense of romance with this. Until I felt like I was going to die from a broken heart. There was definitely no romance in that, only excruciating pain. After the two days went by I can't even explain what happened, but I felt the darkness and the heaviness was lighter. Not gone, but lighter. I felt that there was a sliver of hope that I could get through this eventually. That was the moment the healing process really started.

I forced myself to do things that were difficult but necessary, such as leaving my house. I would contact people in the area and have coffee; I would go to the grocery store for ten minutes at a time; I would cry, I would mourn, I would try to read (even if it was for one minute), I would journal my feelings when I felt I couldn't go on. And there were days I would cry. Progress for me was crying less than eight hours a day, or being able to carry on a conversation for more than five minutes. My exercise was walking because I would throw up if I did anything more strenuous. It took months before I was okay enough to go back to work and even then, I would go into a closet with a box of tissue and cry. It took six months before I realized I could get through this and share bits of my story with others without crying... sometimes.

One of the things I knew I would struggle with was anger. I had gone through a terrible situation a few years before this and I harboured a great deal of anger. It took me four long years, but through meditation, feeling the emotion and letting it go, I finally got through it, and I started to believe I would get through it again. I spent all my free time at the lake, for this is where I felt God closest to me. With every wave that came in, it would take a little bit of stress and sadness with it and leave peace, gratitude, and love. I had to step back and look at the emotion logically. That didn't mean I didn't get angry, because I sure did. But I remembered how I was and how life was when I was angry, and I didn't recognize myself and life wasn't very much fun. You can't operate in a place of love and peace when you are filled with anger and hatred, and I didn't want to stay there. When I had slivers of clarity throughout the day I would enjoy what I could. The lake, friends, family, my support group. I would find gratitude in the simplest things.

Going through the grieving process doesn't mean I don't miss my baby girl. It doesn't mean I am going through life like the death doesn't matter. It means I am living my life the best I can. I will always miss my daughter. I will always have a hole of sadness where she still has that place. It's okay to still cry and have "bad days." There are still times when I miss her so intensely that I shut down for the day and grieve her. But by living my life, I am honoring her memory. I can still hear her say, "Good job, Mom" or "Proud of you, Mom."

You are stronger than you think, and when life seems it will be unbearable to go on God gives you one more ray of hope. He will lift you up and carry you when you need it. He will sit with you in your pain and comfort you like no one else can. He gives you His strength, love, and peace when you have none left.

It's not easy; it's like clawing your way out of a dark well and you are battered, broken, bruised, bleeding, ripped apart, and your soul feels the same way. But you can do it, one baby step at a time.

Two and half months before Bethany died I had studied to be a Life Coach. I had a fulfilling career as a personal trainer and nutrition and wellness consultant, but I was still trying to find my niche. I wanted to guide people through the difficult emotional transitions, but wasn't sure where or how I wanted to do this. After Bethany passed away my niche found me. Life has so many difficult transitions and I am privileged to help people through these transitions. Such things as the death of a loved one, divorce, empty nest, and the transition from being an employee to business owner. I find I have so much more empathy and compassion, but not enough to allow people to stay in the place of being stuck.

I feel as though God has given me a unique perspective on life, how important it is to live it and not to be stuck in the grief or misery. Bethany lived her life, as short as it was, to the fullest, and I want to live mine the same way. She was my hero, and I love her so very much.

I can tell you without a doubt the darkness will subside, a tiny bit at a time. There will again be hope, there will again be happiness and joy. Be kind to yourself and others. You will make it through.

It is my sincerest hope that through my story I can give someone hope that they you too can get through the darkness. Everyone's process is different, so don't compare yourself to others. You too can live your life with power, confidence, and joy. Remember, though life will not be the same, it will be different, you will be different, and your world will be different. Embrace it.

ABOUT THE AUTHOR: Karen Blanchard—better known as "Coach Karen"—is a mother of seven amazing children, as well as a bestselling author, speaker, and coach extraordinaire who specializes in helping people transition through life's most stressful situations with power, confidence, and joy. In addition to her years as a Health and Wellness Coach, Karen brings her firsthand knowledge to every session. She recently found her "calling" after her divorce and the death of her daughter. Karen understands the pain of catastrophic loss and knows the strength it takes to push past it to create joy and happiness once again.

Karen Blanchard
Create Energy Now
createenergynow.com
hello@createenergynow.com
519-440-8061

When the Heart and Soul Speaks

Linda R. McFadden M.Ed, C.Ht

As a young girl of ten, I remember sitting in one of the birch trees in front of our house, staring up at the stars. I would gaze into the night sky, filled with awe and wonder. Yet at the same time, I never really felt that I fit into the world—I tended to see it differently from others. I was lonely.

I remember questioning my purpose, if I had one, and whether or not there was a meaning to life beyond what others considered important. And I wondered whether there was something more and if so, *how on earth would I find it? Where would I even look?*

By age twenty-one I had sustained every type of abuse: emotional, physical, sexual, and psychological. I had fashioned a wall to protect myself and I assumed a mask to hide the pain. What had I done wrong? I tried so hard to be "good". Why couldn't I be happy? I didn't have any answers, I only knew that I desperately needed to find help.

We often wonder why bad things happen; we try to make sense of them. We can find ourselves crying out with the pain of these unanswered questions. It is often when our hearts are broken, when our very selves lay bruised and shattered that we find the answers we seek. Of course, while in the grips of it, we find it nearly impossible to conceive that a blessing is hidden beneath the pain. For that pain can actually be a tool that releases the blessings. In fact, it is one of the primary methods our soul uses to get our attention and break down the barriers in order to connect with us.

There is a story of monks who, hundreds of years ago, encased the solid gold Buddha in mud in order to hide the beloved statue from an invading army that eventually overtook the village and killed all the inhabitants. Years passed and the Buddha's true nature went unrealized, until one day in 1957 a man noticed a glint of gold emanate from a crack in the statue where the mud had chipped off. When he removed the hardened clay he was able to reveal the true nature of the Buddha hidden from view.

And so it is with us. We encase our hearts behind a shield in order to protect it from pain and sorrow. This shield serves as a wall by keeping others out and imprisoning us within. It isn't until we "happen" into a situation where the crack becomes apparent, thereby revealing our hidden true self—a magnificent Being filled with wonder that stretches beyond the limitations of our imagination.

Over thirty years ago, I found my answers in the Christian Church; I caught a powerful glimpse of what I had been searching for and the practical means of obtaining it.

"April 24th?" The Thought sprung into my mind and refused to leave. "What in the world is April 24th?" I asked myself as I scoured my one-bedroom apartment. The only calendar I had was a pocket calendar I carried in my purse. I opened it up—there were no appointments, no clever or moving sayings—nothing that was relevant. But still that Thought persisted.

It had been two years since I had turned my life over to God. I had found the peace, the love. and the joy, as well as the answers I'd been seeking. I had witnessed miracles and was touched by the miraculous.

There was just one thing I believed was missing—a man!

Around that time, I had met the son of an old family friend, and though he lived in another country, my thoughts were filled with him. I had replied to his initial letter with the naïve and desperate dreams of a young woman who wanted to be loved. The silent weeks since I had mailed the letter were weighing on me. Had I come across too needy? Had I made a mistake? Had I just blown my chance for everlasting love? I'd tormented myself with these questions, and now, I was plagued with this seemingly random date, flashing though my mind. April 24th? What in the world did that mean?

It took four days of these consistent thoughts for me to remember the daily, devotional book I had purchased months earlier but had never started to read. I realized that it was dated! I eagerly picked up the book, "Streams in the Desert" by L.B. Cowman, and turned to the date. I don't remember if it was just my jaw that dropped or if I dropped the book as well, but the first line of April 24th devotional stated: "True faith is dropping your letter in the post office box and letting it go."

Several years later, overwhelmed with pain and betrayal, I closed the door on my beliefs and on God altogether. I didn't end up taking my life that night but, with tears flowing and sobs racking my body, I did turn my back on religion and retreated into the safe world of academia.

"What do you mean you are only submitting your application to one university?" my astonished and rather perplexed friends asked. "You have to apply to at least five or six in case you don't get in to the one you want." I didn't listen. I KNEW that if I was going to help others heal, I had to go to the best graduate program, with the highest level of training. I had also identified the university and knew where I needed to go. Six months later, I stood in the elevator of my apartment and smiled as I tore open the acceptance envelope.

Even though on a conscious level I avoided all things spiritual, I could never completely leave behind what I knew to be true. My Soul stood fast, nudging me as I unknowingly gathered what I would need to fulfill my purpose. My "ducking and dodging" eventually led me into a direction that I had never considered and had absolutely zero interest in: metaphysics.

It wasn't that I didn't believe; I had simply never had exposure to it. Yet I had seen too much by then to rule anything out. There is a spiritual law that states when anything comes into my world three times I need to pay attention—that the Universe is attempting to communicate with me. Now, through this law, I was being directed to step outside my comfort zone. I quickly found myself standing outside a well-respected psychic's office. An hour later, I emerged, took a breath and wondered what in the world I had just stepped into?

Life Between Lives therapy? What was that? Was it like "reincarnation"? That was pretty "woo-woo"—even for me. But the message from the psychic was loud and clear. So, adopting a rather scholastic attitude I tentatively dipped my toe into yet another fascinating new world.

I researched, and read, and researched some more. My academic background demanded that I only research those who held accreditation and I found myself studying Dr. Brian Weiss. After six days, when my brain was fried and I needed a rest, I finally turned on the television. There, on the screen, the title of the documentary was displayed: "Past life Regression with Brian Weiss." I physically took a step back and, completely convinced I was on the right path, allowed my life to take another turn.

He had come in for smoking cessation. During the initial interview, I noted that he had a chronic complaint of pain that radiated from beside his belly button around to the same location on his back. MRI's, CT Scans, and innumerable visits to his physician left both him and his doctor puzzled. No identifiable cause translated into "you'll just have to live with it." He was open to the suggestion of a Past Life Regression. He was one of my very first cases.

"Look down at your feet," I directed, "and tell me—what are

you wearing?"
"Boots," he replied. "Black boots."
"Where are you?" "I'm on a field—a battlefield...But I don't
want to be here. I want to be home with my wife and children." He
added, "I don't believe in this war. I'm angry."
"Move ahead in time," I prompted, "What happens next?"
Silence filled the room until he spoke again:
"Ah. I'm dying. I was stabbed in the back with—like a sabre or
something—the point is sticking out in front of me."
"How do you feel about dying? On this day? At this time?"
"I'm so angry at myself," he repeated. "I didn't want to be
here. I didn't want to die."

This client, who had never "believed" or even thought about Past Lives, experienced an astonishing result: the pain he had lived with for years simply vanished. When the anger and the resentment that he had carried into this lifetime was released, the effect was immediate. I had read and researched the possible benefits of past life regression, but after witnessing it firsthand I was amazed.

Oftentimes we turn a corner only to find the doorway to growth, expansion, and healing. When two people meet at this door, it can bring incredible results neither could have foreseen or planned. Synchronicity often steps beyond logical, methodical plans and, as Pascal infamously said, "The heart has its reason which reason doesn't understand."

The psychic had also specifically directly me toward "Life Between Lives" therapy, which led me beyond reincarnation into the fascinating work of Dr. Michael Newton's, "Journey of the Soul." Another door, another step...

Alice was pretty, slim, intelligent, and very depressed. "I've always been depressed," she confided. "I think I was born that way." Countless hours of therapy had left her feeling hopeless and defeated. I recommended a Spiritual Regression (Life Between

Lives) session, and she agreed.

"I didn't want to come to earth," she whispered. "I didn't think it would be this hard."

"What is it that you find 'hard' about the earth incarnation?" I asked.

"This planet is so dense. My body feels so heavy and ... none of my friends are here. I feel so lonely."

"Have you incarnated on other planets before?"

"Yes. The planet was red and I swam . . . like a dolphin . . . but I could also float in the air," she continued in a hush, amazed voice. "I loved it there. . . That's why I am so sad. That's why I am depressed."

"Is there anything else?" I prompted.

Her reply came swift and sure "No. I'm done. I understand now. I can come back . . ."

When I followed up with her three months later, she had quit smoking, started working out and—most importantly—her depression had disappeared. She was happy and at peace!

From thoughts, to nudges and signposts (and even 2X4s when necessary!) we follow the clues picking up bits and pieces that leads us to the discovery of the gold which is always within. I found that the path is winding and fraught with scrapes, bruises, and seemingly intolerable pain that contributes to the fullness, the complexity, and the wonder of our journey.

I've been immersed in the traditional Christian approach, Energy work, Eastern mysticism, Chakras, Native teachings, and Spiritual regressions. I've learned the incredible value inherent in each. Level by level, I have been brought into a new awareness and understanding. I have learned how to blend my earlier spiritual experiences into my evolving understanding of different approaches. I am amazed at the complexity of our own Soul—as well as its very simplicity.

I still look up and gaze at the stars and they still fill me with wonder. Connected to All, I am convinced that we are all the same but different aspects of the Creator—seemingly separate, yet radiating outwards and energetically vibrating as a part of an infinite, unifying field. A field put in motion—fueled by the energy—of both the Heart and the Soul.

ABOUT THE AUTHOR: With a master's degree in Psychology and certified as a Hypnotherapist, Regressionist, and Relationship Therapist, Linda McFadden offers more than thirty years of traditional experience combined with her role as a Coach and a Mystic. This formalized education—along with the insight, wisdom, and practical and spiritual tools she's accumulated— serves to help empower others to take control of their journey and move forward into the life that they desire. Linda's clients are Coaches, Physicians, Ministers, Psychologists, Thought Leaders, and Entrepreneurs.

Linda R. McFadden M.Ed, C.Ht
lindamcfadden.ca
thescienceandthesoul.ca
linda@lindamcfadden.ca
705-741-8921

The Long Road to Loving Myself

Marla Goldberg

Have you ever wondered what it would feel like to live a life of fulfillment, joy, and happiness? If you have, you're not alone. You have also—whether you realize it or not—been guided to read this, just as I was guided to write it. For I too yearned to live that way, and now I do. Part of my mission is to share my story with others in the hopes of helping them be their best selves.

For many years, that story was about an uphill battle, with many twists and turns, many highs and oh, so many lows. It wasn't until I stepped through what I now know is a one-way door down my spiritual path that I learned how to heal others and myself.

My early life was a combination of chaos and isolation. My parents' relationship was "challenged," which is to say they fought constantly. When they weren't fighting or working, they were holed up in their bedroom watching TV, which meant they did not interact much with me or my siblings. So consumed were they with their own disappointments, pain, and challenges, they left us to figure a lot of things out for ourselves. If someone asked me to describe my childhood in two words, neglect and abandonment would immediately spring to mind.

Due to the lack of structure, my brother, sister, and I were constantly fighting as well. It was a difficult way to grow up. I left for school each morning with tearstains on my cheeks, never realizing that not everyone started their day out crying. To me, it was normal.

There was one bright spot during that difficult time: Emmaline. She was hired to watch me and help maintain the house, but she turned out to be my angel. Emmaline loved me and protected me like a mother would. She taught me that there was much more to life than what was going on our house, for which I will be eternally grateful.

Though my parents—both professionals—were well educated, they did not nurture or guide our education. Instead, I became very streetwise, learning from trial and error how to attain what I needed. I started cooking at the age of seven and at the age of fourteen got my first job. I loved working. I loved having money of my own, so much so that by the time I was sixteen I held down two jobs.

Around that time I met my first love. After several years and several agonizing breakups and makeups, he proposed. Just when I was thinking I may get my fairytale after all, everything fell apart. Devastated, I fell into an unhealthy pattern rooted in unworthiness and a low sense of self. If you met me on the street, you wouldn't have seen those traits, but if you followed my choices, it was very evident. These choices—usually around relationships—repeatedly resulted in feelings of shame, disappointment, and rejection. I always felt as though I was just not good enough.

The greatest evidence of my dislike for myself was my decision to marry my first husband. We'd dated briefly when I was eighteen, then reconnected twenty years later. By that time he had lost his wife to a brain aneurysm and was raising two young boys on his own. He also had a drinking problem. Perhaps it was due to my own turbulent childhood, but soon after meeting his kids I knew they were travelling their own rough road of neglect and abandonment. They had been given no counselling to deal with their mother's loss, and their father was in rehab, trying to break his alcohol addiction.

It was because of those boys that I went through with the marriage. By then I had discovered that despite his best attempts to hide it, my future husband was a full-fledged alcoholic and a very mean one at that. If I walked away from those boys, I felt I'd be leaving them to the same fate I'd suffered growing up. Instead, I decided I would stay and be their "Emmaline."

By 2003, I was at the lowest point in my life. I had been married to my abusive husband for seven years, and I was basically raising the children—who I had legally adopted—on my own. I didn't know where to turn or who to turn to, and that's when an opportunity presented itself in the form of a women's conference.

That day, while looking over the topics, the words "How to Heal Yourself" hit me like a bunch of flashing lights. I went to the lecture and everything the woman talked about resonated with me. I signed up for her basic class, never in a million years imagining I was about to have my first psychic experience.

We paired up for an exercise in which one person was the "giver" and the other was the "receiver." When it was my turn to be the receiver, I was so worried about disappointing my partner that I kept repeating, "Please give me something. Please give me something" over and over in my head. Sure enough, I got not one vision, but three: I saw a braid, followed by the braid turning into a rope bridge, then little hands playing a piano.

Then it was time to tell my partner what I had seen. My partner had beautiful long hair, and when I shared my visions with her, she revealed that she had a ritual of growing her hair long, then going to a wooded area near her home where she would cut the braid off and start all over again. She also confirmed that in a former home she had to cross over a rope bridge whenever she walked to town. She confirmed the third vision as well, sharing that she had two small children and was teaching them to play the piano, which was one of the few pieces of furniture they had in their home.

I was both shocked and exhilarated. I had always wanted to be able to knowingly receive guidance, but I was so stuck in my head I didn't know how to connect with Spirit. Now that it had happened, I was hooked!

I enrolled at Inner Focus, AlexSandra Parness's mystery school. For the next three years we met three times a year for a five-day intensive, during which I was trained in fourteen healing/clearing techniques.

AlexSandra's students were also required to work on their own issues. We needed to clean out our closet before we could help someone else clean out theirs. Needless to say, this wasn't an easy process, but as I began to peel back the layers of who I was and how I'd come to be, I learned to forgive myself for the thoughts, decisions, and resulting challenges that hadn't served me, and to accept not only the good parts of me, but the perceived negative ones as well. I also learned to forgive others for their actions that had brought me pain and subconsciously guided my path.

Finally, I also found the strength and courage to file for divorce. He made it as brutal as possible, prolonging the proceedings as long as he could and berating me constantly with phone calls and text messages. It took three years, but at the end of it I was free at last!

After I graduated, I didn't intend to practice what I learned outside a small group of family and friends, so I was surprised when new learning opportunities opened themselves to me. To date I have been trained in over twenty healing/clearing techniques.

In 2008, Gary, a man I'd gone to high school with, reached out to me on Facebook. Though I accepted the friend request I was a bit puzzled. Other than sharing a kiss at fifteen we'd never even had a conversation.

He started instant messaging me, then calling. At the time I had recently ended another relationship, so when Gary asked me to dinner, I said yes.

It turned out to be one of the worst dates I had ever been on! He was so stiff and boring and didn't seem to be having a good time, so when he asked me to lunch the next day I was shocked. For some reason, I was also curious, and since I didn't have anything scheduled I once again accepted.

The second date was only slightly better, yet he asked me out once again. It was around his birthday, and when I offered to treat, he replied that he wanted something else. It was a kiss, and it was the best of my life. The rest, as they say, is history—he proposed in 2010 and we married the following year. As Gary says, he is my *ichiban*—number one in Japanese—and he is.

One morning in 2014, I heard a booming voice in my ear telling me to start a practice and help others "find the love and joy as you found it." When I told Gary about my experience, he agreed it was time.

In creating my practice, I chose what I felt were the most powerful techniques I had learned; Spiritual Response Therapy (SRT), Chinese Face Reading (CFR) Space Clearing, and Intuitive Life Coaching. Since then, I have been using them to help my clients achieve the best lives they can imagine.

At the time of this writing, I found the following poem and was guided to share it. I hope it resonates with you as it does with me.

As I Begin To Love Myself
Gabriel Gonsalves

As I begin to love myself I found that anguish and emotional suffering as only warning signs that I was living against my own truth. Today I know, this is AUTHENTICITY.

As I begin to love myself I understood how much it can

offend somebody if I try to force my desires on this person, even though I knew the time was not right and the person was not ready for it, and even though this person was me. Today I call it RESPECT.

As I began to love myself I stopped craving for a different life, and I could see that everything that surrounded me was inviting me to grow. Today I call it MATURITY.

As I began to love myself I understood that at any circumstance, I am in the right place at the right time, and everything happens at the exactly right moment. So I could be calm. Today I call it SELF-CONFIDENCE.

As I began to love myself I freed myself of anything that is no good for my health—food, people, things, situations, and everything that drew me down and away from myself. At first I called this attitude a healthy egoism. Today I know it is LOVE OF ONESELF.

As I began to love myself I quit trying to always be right, and ever since I was wrong less of the time. Today I discovered that it is MODESTY.

As I began to love myself I refused to go on living in the past and worrying about the future. Now, I only live for the moment, where everything is happening. Today I live each day, day by day, and I call it FULFILLMENT.

As I began to love myself I recognized that my mind can disturb me and it can make me sick. But as I connected it to my heart, my mind became a valuable ally. Today I call this connection WISDOM OF THE HEART.

We no longer need to fear arguments, confrontations, or any kind of problems with others or ourselves. Even stars collide, and out of their crashing new worlds are born. Today I know THAT IS LIFE!

These days, I live with an open and loving heart. I love guiding and supporting those who are in a place that is not serving them. I love knowing that all I endured was not in vain, but can he used to help others.

We are all Divine beings brought here to learn, teach, grow, love, and to be loved. Show Spirit that you have shown up by loving yourself from the inside out. You won't regret it.

ABOUT THE AUTHOR: Marla Goldberg is an Energy Healer, Intuitive, Author, Speaker, and Host of Guided Spirit Conversations podcast. Marla began her spiritual education in 2003 when she attended her first Mystery School. During her time in school, Marla was trained in fourteen healing modalities. Since graduating, Marla embraces her spiritual path by continuing her education to help her clients and through her podcast. When Marla is not working, she shares her life with her husband Gary and her two dogs, Mabel and Tug.

Marla Goldberg
Marla Goldberg Energy Healer Au Fait
mghealer.com
marla@mghealer.com
847-275-5584

From Victim to Victor
Michelle Cole

To successfully move from victim to victor, you have to truly embrace what insecurity is. After a twenty-year journey of deep and rocky self-reflection, I can say I am now brave enough to accept the true meaning of insecurity. Insecurity results from placing yourself at the center of every interaction you have and then feeling "less-than" because others are not in agreement with your take on things. Simply put, you are relying on the approval of others to attain your self-confidence. For years, I defined my inadequacy by the way others treated me. However, it is when you reach beyond yourself that the true meaning of insecurity is found, is healed, and can be seen as a magical tool for transformation. The true path to self-confidence lies in doing things that impress yourself—not others. But before you can impress yourself, you have to know yourself—who you are, what you stand for, what makes you feel good, and what does not.

Ironically, the curiosity that drove me to find out what was "wrong" with me, led me to discover that nothing was. The only thing "wrong" was the judgement of myself and others. By learning more about myself, I was able to heal. When I started to heal, I held less judgement of myself. As I held less judgement, I became softer in my interactions with others. From a very early age, I felt like I didn't belong and like something was wrong with me. I know now I am an HSP (Highly Sensitive Person) and an Empath, but at the time, I didn't know these labels. Highly Sensitive Persons (HSPs) are born with highly sensitive nervous systems that allow them to grasp subtle changes in energy in both the emotional and physical environment. This makes them become overwhelmed by the emotional distress of others or in highly stimulating environments. Empaths can actually feel others' energy so fiercely they often mistake the energy as their own. This leads to depression and not trusting yourself because you are constantly confused between what are your feelings as opposed to what are others'. Because I was so sensitive, I was subject to years of bullying and being made fun of. As I grew, so did my lack of confidence. And this lack of self-confidence led me to make many poor choices well into my adult life. I felt like life was happening to me, instead of my being in charge of my life circumstances.

Children so sensitive to energy are often wrongly being labeled as hyper-sensitive and often asked why they can't just be like everybody else. Since they represent a mere twenty percent of the population, they most definitely are not like everybody else. From an early age, they can develop self-confidence issues if they don't learn to see their sensitivity as a gift. Since children create a sense of self-worth during their early formative years, it is important for parents of these children to realize their child needs more help creating self-confidence than the "average" child.

Finding out my "labels" was encouraging, but I needed more than just knowledge; I also needed to take action. I reached a point in my life where I could no longer play the victim. One day while I was meditating, I received the message that the only way to change was to admit that I was the only common denominator in all of my life's drama. No matter how horrible I felt and how hard it was to face, I had to accept that fact, or nothing in my life could change. Taking responsibility for the things that happen in your life is the first step in reclaiming your personal power. It takes you from victim to victor in a flat second.

The groundwork lies in the understanding that we are all here to grow and learn. Each life experience we have is an opportunity for growing up spiritually. To expand our vision beyond ourselves to something larger than our egos and our personalities is our work here. Each of us have our own personal journey. Knowing this, we can start to see that we don't need to take our interactions with others personally—as something they are doing to us. The numerous types of scenarios played out with various types of people at different times in our lives are there to assist us in our transformation. We learn from experience, and that experience is had through interaction with others. This is how we learn what does and what does not work for us, which beliefs we can hang onto, and which are outdated and need to be let go.

However, if we continue to see ourselves as victims, by Law of Attraction we will keep attracting the same until we shift our perspective. As a child, I grew to believe that I was unlovable because I was so different. This led me to attract friends who did not treat me with respect, and to several emotionally abusive relationships where I was controlled or used. All of this gave me evidence to back up my "story" of being unlovable.

One of the harder lessons I had to learn was that no matter how much someone may have harmed me or done me wrong, I still have to own a percentage of that experience. Even if that percentage is merely .000001%, I was still involved in the interaction. I had to admit that I did not love myself and I was attracting people who reflected that. I realized that if I could just get past what had happened *to me* and see how I could use these experiences *for me*—to develop self-love—my life could change for the better. I learned I actually held the power all along. I just had to shift how I approached life. Through many spiritual and personal development teachings, I learned how the power of my mind and the power of my thoughts created my life experiences. I became so excited with what I had learned that I wanted to share it with others. I'd been coaching people all my life. Friends and even strangers would tell me their problems and I instinctively knew the right thing to say, not only to comfort them but to lead them in the direction of personal empowerment. So, I decided to make it official and took the proper training to get certified as a life coach.

In 2014, I started coaching adult clients. Many of them had stories similar to mine—they felt they didn't have what it took to accomplish their dreams because they had not been taught the principles of Emotional Intelligence. Emotional Intelligence (EQ) is defined as the ability to recognize, evaluate, and regulate your own emotions, as well as the emotions of those around you. Our society tends to solely focus on IQ, but EQ is just as important. As we become more conscious of how our emotions drive our behavior, we can then make changes to our behavior, for our betterment.

One day, I found a quote from Frederick Douglass—"It is easier to build strong children than to repair broken men." It became apparent to me that my true passion was to teach children life skills that foster self-confidence. I wanted to teach them about personal power early on. With self-confidence, children can learn how to make decisions without peer pressure playing a role. They can learn how to handle the unexpected turns in life. They can learn how to take responsibility for creating their own lives. Self-confident children are children who believe in themselves and their dreams. They are the master of their own lives, rather than simply accepting what life handed them. Of course life is not without conflict, but given the right tools, it does not have to become a debilitating ordeal where you spend more time healing from events than learning and growing from them.

In order to fulfill this mission of teaching children to be self-confident, it was important for me to receive proper training in the field of personal development. I wanted to teach not preach! I became certified by Coach U and began to use the WISDOM curriculum as my medium to teach life skills based in emotional development. The Adventures in Wisdom Life Coaching Program for Kids™ is a fun, story-based program that gives step-by-step tools for helping kids learn how to handle the ups and downs of growing up, to think for themselves and make good decisions, and to go for their dreams and make them happen. It teaches children how to train their conscious, subconscious, and superconscious minds in order to be in charge of their own lives instead of feeling like life is happening to them.

For those who don't know, let me explain these three "minds."

The **Conscious Mind** is our thinking mind, which sees life as it appears to be. We train it to either see life in a positive light or a negative one. If the Conscious Mind is the pilot, the **Subconscious Mind** is the copilot, the silent listener. It is the part of our mind where what we feel deeply is impressed. The subconscious mind is so powerful that it can sabotage our conscious intentions if we don't program it correctly, with positive thoughts and actions. Not all things, however, can be accomplished through the conscious and the subconscious minds. And that is when we call upon our **Superconscious Mind**. This is the God mind, or Spirit mind (whichever makes you most comfortable). This is your Higher Self, which knows your exact purpose and lives in the realm of perfect ideas. This mind operates by intuition, defined as the ability to understand something immediately, without the need for conscious reasoning.

In addition to Coach U and the WISDOM curriculum, I use my gifts as an Intuitive and Reiki Energy Healer in conjunction with the personal development training to offer a full program of mind and body awareness. I also developed a program called REAP Your EQ. REAP stands for Request assistance, Express commitment, Accept guidance, and track your Progress. It is a four-step process that teaches children the skills of discerning between the ego's voice of fear and your spirit's voice of guidance and love. This discernment allows them to make decisions from a place of empowerment, not from a reactionary place of fear.

My coaching practice is unique because I teach both intellectual and intuitive skills to foster self-confidence. The WISDOM curriculum teaches children how to use the power of their minds and the power of their thoughts to create self-confidence, and my REAP program teaches them how to reclaim their personal power by tapping into their intuition for daily guidance, thus learning to turn obstacles into growth opportunities. After all, we are spiritual beings having a physical experience— not the other way around, like most of us believe! Once upon a time, I was that highly sensitive kid and I've learned how to heal from my life experiences and see my sensitivity for the gift that it is. Now, my passion is to give the "cliff notes" to kids so then can enjoy this beautiful life exactly how they were made—perfectly and with nothing to fix!

Once you start taking responsibility for your life and no longer seek to place the blame outside of yourself, two things happen. First and foremost, you become empowered to make choices from the confident stance of who you really are. Second, you gain compassion for your fellow man, knowing they are on their own personal journey as well. Then, you can choose discernment over judgment and decide if that person or that circumstance should be a part of your life. I firmly believe the simple act of gaining self-confidence can change the energy of the world and that we can work towards living in peace because we are living from our authentic being. To heal and harness self-confidence in the adults of tomorrow is my honor.

ABOUT THE AUTHOR: For many years, Michelle Cole saw the world as a place where things were constantly happening *to her*. Her life forever changed when she stopped looking at her life through the lens of being a victim. She began to see what these life experiences had done *for her*, rather than *to her*. These "obstacles" were opportunities, directing her towards self-confidence. Her healing journey led to her life's purpose—teaching children life skills that foster self-confidence. With self-confidence, children learn how to take responsibility for creating their own lives. As a Kid's Life Skills Coach, Michelle Cole would be honored to share her experience and training with your family.

Michelle Cole
Be Brave, Be You!
BeBraveBeYou.org
Michelle@BeBraveBeYou.org
404-323-5376

Reclaiming the Power of Soul Guidance
Julia Mikk

Self Doubt

From a very young age I was embroiled in a constant struggle to be some unrealistic idea of what I thought I should be. My teen years in my hometown in Estonia were an emotional rollercoaster of desperately trying to fit in, feeling depressed, inadequate, and painfully alone. My parents' divorce when I was thirteen only made me even more insecure and confused. Certain that I wasn't pretty enough or thin enough, I dieted and exercised until I was terribly underweight. Still, when I looked in the mirror, all I saw was a fat girl. Looking back, it's such a striking lesson in the power of perception!

By eighteen, I had lost so much weight that my menstrual cycle stopped completely. The turning point was a stern warning I received from an acupuncturist: if I continued to lose weight my body would lose the ability to have children! I don't know if it was true or he was only trying to scare me, but his words broke the spell of "Not thin enough!" I was able to stop my anorexic behavior, though the crippling insecurity remained.

A New Land

While at University, I learned about an opportunity to study and work in Ireland for a year. This was my chance to get away from my family and hometown, gain my freedom, and learn English, and I seized it.

When I arrived in the small, lush Irish town where I was to study and work as a waitress, I felt as if *finally* I was standing on my own in the world. And for a short while, everything felt new and exciting.

But the dogged inner pressure to be perfect and be liked came crushing back. I may have been living in Ireland, but the noise in my head sounded the same as it had in Estonia. I felt lost and out of place, except now there was neither family nor friends to comfort me. I was utterly alone.

No More!

Then one day after one of my regular crying bouts, a voice within me proclaimed, "No more!" I had been walking home to my cheap little motel room, and right there in the street something in me screamed, "I am done with this suffering! There must be a way out of this!"

The inner voice felt wise, protective, and caring. It was strong, and powerful, and the message was unmistakable: *You can change. You deserve better!*

Though I lacked the words to explain it, somehow I trusted this mysterious voice that arose from deep inside of me.

Within a couple of weeks, I went to the restaurant where I worked, and with a trembling voice told the owners I was quitting. Somehow, I stood up to their threat to contact my University and have me kicked out of school. I still walked away.

With this mysterious inner guidance prodding me, I headed to Dublin, a vibrant, cultured city completely different from the village where I'd spent the past six months. On one of my first days there, while perusing a paper in a café, I came across an ad for a restaurant manager. I'd never managed a restaurant—or anything else for that matter—yet again, that wise voice inside, prodded me: "Go for it!" So, I did, and to my surprise, I was hired. They probably saw me as cheap labor, but it was more money than I'd made in my life!

The restaurant was called Samsara, a Sanskrit word that refers to a wheel of suffering. In retrospect, it was a perfect reference to my own confusion and agitation.

Samsara

Is it any wonder that while working at Samsara, I fell deeper into a personal samsara of drinking, smoking, and partying? I had no clue how to deal with my inner suffering so instead I pretended I was happy. The parties and drinking were an enjoyable distraction and lifted my spirits—at least for a while.

I was also suddenly receiving a lot of attention from men, fulfilling a dream I'd harbored since childhood: to be adored by the opposite sex.

For the first time in my life, I possessed everything I thought I'd wanted: I was thin, earning more money than ever before, free to live my life on my own terms in a city I loved. Men liked me, and I felt sexy. Yet, something was still missing.

A few months later, a sudden moment of awakening came over me. I realized that while "I had absolutely everything I ever dreamt of" I was still completely unhappy!

How could this be?

It was one of the most perplexing moments of my life.

It made me ask myself, "Well, what else is there? What would bring me happiness if all this doesn't?"

Go Explore!

Step by step, in ways large and small, a new world began to reveal itself. I found and devoured the books *The Alchemist* and *The Celestine Prophecy,* both of which completely changed my world. Something in me opened. Something I had known when I was little had returned full force. Something very strong, deeply curious, and also profoundly satisfying was calling me to explore. I stopped drinking, smoking, and eating meat. I started inquiring what my life was really about.

It was around that time that my work-study program ended. After twelve months in Ireland, I was going home.

Spiritual Breathing

Back in Estonia, I dove into all kinds of healing modalities, yoga, meditations, talking to Angels, healing, chakras… you name it. Anything that sounded spiritual, I went for it. My thirst was so great. I think of it as a pull to Grace. Something much greater than me took charge of my life.

A major turning point was a weekend workshop on a modality called Spiritual Breathing. Friends told me a well-known teacher from America was facilitating the event. It was a special opportunity.

Seated in a large room with fifty students, I learned how the breath was connected to our subconscious and how working with the breath in a specific way, one could access the subconscious in ways that even psychotherapy can't, liberating it from unresolved pain and limitations in the most powerful of ways.

But it was my direct experience with the power of Spiritual Breathing that completely pulled me out of my trance of suffering. One two-hour workshop opened my heart and understanding in ways that nothing else ever had. I woke up to seeing everything as pure love and grace. I felt a connectedness, oneness, and pure unlimited peace—not as a theory, but as my own innermost reality.

It was like a rebirth. A new Julia was born.

Each subsequent workshop anchored this awareness more and more in my nervous system. Each session, enriched each tiny cell with new information about love, grace, and an unbounded sense of well-being.

Soon after that my Inner Guidance guided me to Gangaji, another American spiritual teacher. Sitting with her at her week-long retreat everything changed again. She invited us to simply stop.

"There is nothing to do, nowhere to go, nothing to accomplish. Everything you want is already here, right now, completely available," she explained. "Just be still enough to become aware of it."

That blew my mind completely open! All of a sudden all I knew was a pure silence filled with peace, ease, rest, and the knowing that all is completely well. Julia with all her fears, desires, worries, accomplishments, even her spiritual search, was just a character of my imagination, a construct of my mind. Wow.

If I am not who I thought I was, who am I really?

This was the question that started emanating from my being every day.

Suddenly I found myself in love—in love with every cell of my body. In love with every instant of life. No matter how mundane it was or ordinary, I was fascinated by it. My breath was like my lover. And, every hair on my body was like a little miracle.

It added a whole new dimension to my work with consciousness, and I ended up calling it Breath of Love because it was about living in Love, Freedom, and Pure Presence that was our innermost nature.

One year later, my Inner Guidance prodded me to take a new leap and move to the U.S. At first this made no sense to me. I loved my life in Estonia, with a promising career and wonderful friends. Yet the voice inside was crystal clear. *Go to the U.S.!*

I remembered that my American Spiritual teacher had once taught a workshop on the power of Intuition, and told the audience that if an inner calling seemed irrational it was most likely the voice of our Higher Self guiding us. It was our bigger life purpose calling us. The very fact that it was irrational meant this was something much bigger than our analytical mind or our limited life experience. With that, my decision was made.

When I arrived in the US I allowed myself to be led, literally from one moment to the next. Before I knew it, I was living in New

Orleans, opened my Breath of Love healing practice, made new wonderful friends, and thoroughly enjoyed the rich local culture.

Breath of Love

Before long, I was sharing my Breath of Love work on a bigger scale, giving workshops all over the country, and offering private sessions to those who wanted to go deeper. People invited me to their cities, offered to organize workshops for me, and shared their houses when I visited. Something greater than myself was carrying me from one abundant opportunity to another.

About six months after I arrived in New Orleans, my Inner Guidance suddenly told me to leave the city and go to Ashland, Oregon *immediately*. This seemed like the strangest guidance! I'd barely heard of Ashland, Oregon. Plus, I very much loved my life in New Orleans. There was no reason to leave. Once again remembering the wisdom of the "irrational" intuition, I packed my bags, said goodbye to my dear friends, and left.

Thirty days later, the reason for the guidance was revealed. My old home in New Orleans had been hit by Hurricane Katrina and was completely demolished! There were many deaths and people missing, yet for some reason I had been saved. I fell to my knees, eyes welling with tears of gratitude.

In that moment I fell into an even deeper devotion for my Inner Guidance. This Presence that was guiding me was clearly, infinitely bigger, and wiser than my little mind. It knew how to protect and guide me perfectly. I just had to listen.

Ever since then my Breath of Love work became imbued with the inspiration to help others find that deep inner guidance too— letting them find their inner guru, their inner Spiritual Teacher, their pure connection to Source and ability to follow their most sacred purpose in life.

For many people listening to that clear inner guidance was not easy; there was too much noise in their mind, covering up the wisdom of their Spirit.

A lot of my work became about peeling away those layers of fear and unresolved hurt that were in the way, and the more I facilitated it, the more I saw the proof of the benevolence, intelligence, and wisdom of our innermost spiritual nature. There were many Breath of Love sessions where old chronic pain (including the kind of pain that no doctor could previously alleviate) completely disappeared. There were others where old unresolved trauma that no other psychotherapist could heal, completely healed.

And, what I loved the most was seeing how once the shift happened inside, it was immediately reflected in my client's external reality.

I am still fascinated by this work, even after eighteen years. When people heal their old trauma, let go of inner blocks, and start listening to their inner guidance their outer life immediately changes too. All of a sudden new abundance comes into their lives, exciting financial opportunities show up, deeply satisfying relationships come along, and most importantly—living their most sacred purpose becomes easy and grace-filled. It all begins with listening to the wise voice inside.

ABOUT THE AUTHOR: Julia Mikk, born in Estonia and now living in America, is an internationally renowned teacher and facilitator, and founder of Breath of Love work. Julia's sessions instantly change lives. Over the past eighteen years she has worked with thousands of people who come from all over the world to experience the power of Breath of Love process, undergo transformation, and embody courage to live their soul purpose.

Julia Mikk
Breath of Love
BreathofLove.org
julia@breathoflove.org

All Dressed Up & No Place to Go
Christine Clark

The metaphorical image I have of the early years of my life's journey is of me, inside a small opaque balloon with a bouquet of smaller, multi-colored balloons clutched in one hand. My other hand was free so I could multitask through my survival codes that were established before my birth.

The balloon I was contained in served as a challenge to connect with others and my environment. The bouquet of balloons I held were to be the challenging experiences I would use to help me find out who I really was, through the unlearning of who I *thought* I was.

From inside my balloon, the sounds of the world were always muffled; I always felt all dressed up with no place to go while watching and wondering how everyone else was finding the party. People always seemed headed somewhere, but nobody was inviting me or telling me how to get there. It was literally like being too small for people to see me or notice I was there.

I never wanted to follow other people's breadcrumbs and I never left my own breadcrumbs to track where I had been. This left less options and forced me to move in only one direction, which was straight ahead.

I arrived with a lung infection so severe I almost didn't make it. This would become a pattern of my body taking on strange but survivable illnesses. Both ears were constantly infected, which affected my hearing and explained the muffled sounds I heard—both metaphorically and physically—throughout my life. It was the 1960s—when many of my ailments were still a mystery—and my poor parents had no idea what to do with a child who was always sick. I would eventually develop great compassion for them, but first I had to move into compassion for myself.

As it turned out, I had chosen the perfect family to learn how to do this. My childhood was a very challenging one—from the age of two to six I was molested by my grandfather, and when I was with my parents I was mostly left alone, expected to never be seen or heard. Like most children, I had endless energy and a very vivid imagination that included a dear friend nobody else could see or hear. And, like many children, I was labeled "hyperactive" and at the age of three put on a drug called Ritalin. Suddenly, I could no longer see or hear my friend! Eventually, my parents took me off the drug because of the side effects, but my friend never returned.

Things only got harder when I started school. I was teased for being "different," and despite repeated tests, no one could figure out why I was not understanding things. It never occurred to them that all I needed was someone to spend time teaching me. Isolated both at home and at school, I began to feel left out and even shunned. I began to believe I was stupid and not as good as others.

What saved me was my love for reading. I started to feel more confident and by grade six I was scoring at the top percentiles on province-wide exams testing mechanical reasoning. Yet I still harbored feelings of anger toward myself for "letting" the abuse happen. I developed a drinking problem that lasted thirty years and often consumed my every waking moment.

Despite my physical challenges, I still managed to be an amazing athlete. It seems that I was always living the extremes— if I was not in bed with an illness, I was turning everything I touched, athletically speaking, into gold. At fifteen, I spent a month in Oregon for the Olympic track training trials. When I finally returned to the town where we lived, I was expecting to see my parents there to pick me up, only to find myself waiting alone. Crushed, I had to beg a complete stranger for a ride home. My parents were at a party and had forgotten about me! It brought to mind the painful memory of my mother not being there to pick me up after my first day of kindergarten. I waited forever, then finally started walking home, only to get lost. A babysitter noticed me wondering around in another neighborhood and brought me home.

A year after the Olympic trials, I was raped by my best friend and a week later had landed in the hospital with spinal meningitis. He committed suicide three weeks after that, the same night I was discharged. I didn't stay home for long, though; I had had enough of my parents' drinking and their harsh judgements—not to mention the burden as the oldest of three of having to run the house. For the next three years I worked in the hotel industry, and had a part-time job as a nanny for a family that owned a strippers' agency. Young and taken with idea of being a dancer, I soon found myself travelling throughout British Columbia, believing it was the start of a career in entertainment. Instead, it was the start of my drinking problem. I spent the next two years on the road without a break. I carried the Taiwan flu in my body for six months, was badly beaten by a very large, very scary person who just came out of nowhere, and was raped twice by people I thought were friends. I also negotiated twice for my life with two different chapters of the British Columbia Hell's Angels. To this day I'm not sure how I was able to do that; I just know it was not part of the script to die that way. I was meant to live and bring more life to this world and that is what I did.

I left dancing, got married, and had two beautiful children—a girl and a boy. From the first day, they made it so easy to be their mother. It was like the Universe knew to send in two kids that would be easy to raise so I would be able to catch up on my stunted growth and integrate myself back into society. I raised my children alone without friends or family; I had no connection to the idea of manufacturing or finding "my village" to help. Nobody showed me what to do, and when I divorced my husband, his family dropped me like a hot potato. I was familiar with this pattern and although it hurt, I accepted it as my normal.

That did not mean it was easy. During those years I suffered from depression and post-traumatic stress syndrome and spent a lot of time sleepwalking through my life. Overnight I had become both a single mother and a solo business owner, and I felt isolated and alone. I soon began drinking again—it was my only friend and the only relief from the never-ending stress. Before I knew it my children were in high school, and I felt like I barely knew them.

"A Course in Miracles" would be my saving grace. This book got my attention just long enough to spark my interest and a desire to stay sober enough to comprehend its content. I began to get into the right relationship with myself and understand my drinking. It was not the wine making me sick, but my relationship with it. My body and mind had become so addicted to the drama of my health issues and the drinking just brought on more problems for my body to deal with. Now, I realized I had let this cycle of mental and physical abuse go on long enough. I was ready to choose again.

I then moved on to channel Paul Selig and his Guides, followed by Matt Kahn and his teachings. Because of the parallel patterns in these otherwise very different teachings I was able to move deeper into myself, retrieve my soul, and literally live in my body once again. Because I have a scientific mind I am able to shred through the teachings of Quantum Physics, which helped me to be more grounded and integrated. I can't tell you where the bubble I had been living in went, but it is gone, like a distant memory of another, older me. This new me had returned to my innocence and my sovereign being. There is great power here that is unfolding and I am no longer feeling all dressed up and nowhere to go. Open and exposed means alive. Enlightenment does not mean life does not have challenges; it means you participate with awareness bathed in acceptance and a reverence for life and love. This short-circuits the degree and duration of the suffering and you always see opportunity within it. You choose from your knowing. You grow and lift yourself and by living your life as an example instead of telling everyone else what to do, you lift others as well.

I followed the music with clarity and the muffled sounds were gone. I stopped needing someone to go to the party with and instead started trusting that I could find the party on my own. When I showed up at the party and opened the door, I saw me with the most beautiful balloons I had ever seen, of colors I had never seen before in this life. It was my party and I had written the guest list. I was the party, and everyone in this lifetime who played a role in my awakening was there ... and there was love and laughter.

Another turning point was a Quantum Healing Hypnosis session, where my Higher Self was able to communicate the path to healing. For me, this meant not forcing my perfection on my body, but learning to be gentle and patient towards it, like a wise, trusted elder. My Higher Self also gave me several examples of how I could practice self-care. I'd had many of these ideas in the years prior to the session but never applied, for I did not trust they came from a higher perspective. Now I was stunned at how aligned I already was with my Higher Self and its clear communication to me!

This session also helped me heal through forgiveness, specifically around the sexual abuse. My Higher Self protected me from the details, but allowed me to see how this experience had presented an opportunity to learn. I realized not only that forgiveness was the only answer, but that the first person I had to forgive was myself! For years I had been angry with myself for letting this happen to me and I did not treat myself well because of it.

Since that awakening process I am actually able to go back in time and experience the same moments, not as a victim, but from my higher perspective. I can be a spirit guide to myself and forgive all from a place of knowing that this was scripted for my growth and their growth, including how I played my role as a mother, which freed me from parental guilt and into joyful liberation and purpose. I can even go back and erase all imprinted memories from my body through real forgiveness. Quantum Healing Hypnosis can help you get to the party!

Today I relish in my solitude and dive deep in communion with my soul, yet at the same time I have a deep reverence for community and family and I participate in relationships from a heart-centered place, safe in the knowing what "normal" feels like. I enjoy a more balanced and harmonized experience of myself. Solitude is not the same as loneliness, but rather a connection to all; it is a sense of community and belonging. I am coming from a place of authenticity now, instead of a superficial place and I feel the wholeness of that. I can hear so clearly the sweet melody of Spirit and its gentle, patient, and balanced promptings for my shimmering purpose-filled balloons that I affectionately refer to as my life.

ABOUT THE AUTHOR: Christine Clark has been involved in the Fitness/Nutrition and Healing Arts for twenty-five years. She is the founder of Pilates Fusion Inc., where she provides a unique, sacred space for healings of all kinds to occur. She is also a Licensed Naturopath; Ayurvedic Consultant; Advanced Reiki / Integrated Energy Therapist; Reconnective Healing Practitioner / The Reconnection; Therapeutic Massage Therapist and Hypnotist. Currently, Christine is focused on the work of Delores Cannon and is a QHHT Practitioner, helping people to communicate with their Higher Self and their Interdimensional natural state of being, to facilitate acceptance of their human form with more Love and Joy.

Christine Clark
Hypnosis Healing 5D
Hypnosis Healing 5D.ca and .com
clarkchristine9@gmail.com
514-671-9834

Body/Mind/Spirit Alignment
Elaine Belle

I was born in 1950, a time when many cultural values were changing, and many new ways of thinking were starting to come alive and be accepted. It was the beginning of a major transformation, not only in the United States, but across the globe. Still, if someone had told me when I was young what my life would be like I would have never believed them, or thought it was even possible.

I came from a rural, working-class family with definite rules about expressing emotions—or, more accurately, not expressing them. Limitations were an accepted and expected way of life. As a child I left my body as a means of survival. My parents traveled for work, leaving me behind with my grandparents and crazy uncle. It would have been difficult to care for a toddler on the road, and they believed staying with family would be the safest place for me. They had no way of knowing my uncle would molest a two-year-old or that my grandmother's way of "helping me when I was upset" was to give me an enema (this was actually a standard way of thinking for some grandmothers at the time.) Mom just thought I was the "fussiest" of her six children. I shut my feelings off and with them my ability to listen to my body. I was clumsy, spacy, ungrounded and did not make choices from my intuition, even though this part of me was very active.

It took a long time and much training/unlearning to come into and be present to a body filled with sensations of overwhelm and fear. I did not know how my body functioned or why some situations made me sick (though I was always fascinated by what was happening internally). I also didn't understand why people would say one thing and their bodies would be saying something else. I didn't know then that everyone is unique with their own particular path. I thought everyone except me understood how life worked, and that I had not been given the instructions. It was confusing and lonely.

Like many young women growing up in the sixties, I wanted to help others. Nursing seemed like a good opportunity, that is, until I took chemistry in high school. I realized that being a nurse wasn't going to happen. I was dyslexic, which, back then, was completely misunderstood. Not knowing my right from my left was considered a sign of stupidity. No one knew—or at least they didn't explain to me—that I had a different way of learning. In retrospect, I simply had a different approach to processing incoming information, one that would take me many years to understand and appreciate.

In my late teens I embraced hippie culture and wanted to get back to the land.

Doing meditation, yoga, and taking drugs gave me deeper insights to my body and fueled my desire to know more. I liked being able to differentiate organic food from non-organic food by taste. Moreover, eating it seemed like common sense—why would you put things in your body that were used to kill insects?

Being a complex multilayered young woman, it took time and awareness to unwind life-learned habits and patterns. I wanted to understand myself and my place in this world. My way of thinking and understanding did not match most people around me. I still thought everyone else knew what was going on, that somehow I hadn't yet been informed about the way life worked. I didn't understand the heartlessness in the world, how minorities were treated with such lack of caring, or why animals were treated with such cruelty.

On the road to adulthood, it's always comforting when someone is traveling on a similar path as you, and I was lucky enough to find a few. My dear friend Jorna was a soul sister to me. Our lives had parallel traumas, and shared a deep interest in heart-opening experiences. It helped me to have someone exploring the same ideas and giving me a new way to look at them, from different angles. Jorna was extremely sensitive on all levels—body, mind, and spirit. She chose to end her life at age sixty, after many years of illness, and though our thirty years of sharing had ended on the physical plane, I continue to feel her support and sense her spirit when I need her.

When I graduated from college with a degree in education teaching jobs were difficult to find. After a short time in Mexico trying to learn Spanish to become a bilingual teacher I ended up at an ELS School in Los Angeles, teaching students from around the world. As it turned out, my time in LA would provide a pivotal learning experience: I got Rolfed.

Rolfing is a series of deep connective tissue sessions designed to unearth buried emotions. After being so out of my body and avoiding my emotional baggage I was thrust directly into it. I was both fascinated and overwhelmed by what I had unconsciously stored in my body, and though it was a relief to have it come out, I had no support to integrate it. Some days I would wake up crying, other days, laughing. I decided to study Rolfing to get a better understanding of what I was going through. When I was denied acceptance because my physical stature was too small and light for their qualifications, I moved to San Francisco to Study Postural integration. That was where I discovered Alexander work.

My first session resonated to my bones. The Alexander Technique was a much gentler approach to understanding the body/mind and alignment. It helps to understand the relationship of head (one of the heavier parts of the body) to the spine, and moving with direction throughout the body. That means having less compression in the body. With the Alexander technique I learned to think with my whole body, my whole being. To do this is simple on one level but it calls into play unconscious thinking or habits of moving. Examining these habits helps change unhealthy patterns.

I married another body/mind oriented person and settled down to what I thought was going to be my life. When my marriage ended two years later, I moved to New York to study with another Alexander teacher, Thomas Lemens. It was again a time of big change.

My relationships with men had been so difficult, yet no one was more surprised than me when I fell in love with a woman—singer, performer, and teacher Sheilah Glover. Never before had I been in such a supportive, loving relationship. I moved back to the West Coast to be with her, and now, almost thirty years later, we're still together—growing and learning from each other and raising our daughter, Lotus.

Pamela Martin, another dear friend, has helped me remain open to the many ways of finding and understanding the seemingly complex but simple nature of Being. I met Pamela about a year after Sheilah and I adopted Lotus. Over the next two decades, this beautiful soul and gifted psychiatrist has been key in my healing, helping me know how to relate to myself by contacting the place of the Divine, God, Goddess, love within myself. Whatever name one gives it, it all comes back to the same desire, to be the love we are. Pamela also introduced me to the Sedona Method, which has given me more ways to release unconscious beliefs and ways of thinking, opening my heart and, ultimately, resting into love.

I also had another learning path—one that to this day I wish I had not had to go down. It happened back in the 1980s, while I was living in New York. Like many city dwellers, I spent much of my summer in Connecticut, and that's where I contracted Lyme disease. This experience, though highly unpleasant, taught me a tremendous amount about how the body/mind works. I now know that I can only respond to what life presents me, and not resisting what is/was helped me move forward. The illness brought me to yet another level of self-understanding and of seeing the psycho/physical connection to my sense of well-being. I learned that "neurons that fire together wire together." When I was having a flare-up of Lyme symptoms and was exposed to something like mold or pollens my body-mind would put these reactions together. I had become even more sensitive to the environment. The limbic system is important to survival but gets dysregulated. From continual stress and trauma we lose the ability to go from intense reaction/thinking back to the calmness of just being. In the wild, animals seem to keep this regulation—a deer reacts to danger but a short time later goes back to eating with calmness. This is often referred to as the fight-flight mechanism. As humans we are especially challenged now with electronics as well as increasing toxic chemicals in our environment that keep us constantly engaged. We lose the rhythmic flow of excitement to calm, we become dysregulated and this can lead to dis-ease.

I began to realize I was stuck in overdrive, stuck in the sympathetic part of my nervous system, thus wearing down this system, and the adrenals as well. When the system becomes dysregulated, temperature control and normal body functions are put in jeopardy, which in turn makes healing and being calm close to impossible.

When I became aware of my physical reactivity and learned to slow down the reactions I could stay calmer and respond from a more neutral place, even when I was in a highly charged situation. It would take years of work to change the way my limbic system played into my physical reactions, but it changed my life and my ability to relate to others. I could make myself sicker by overreacting to present situations that triggered an emotional response to past traumas. It is a fine line to walk and takes willingness not to believe everything I think. Becoming aware of the unconscious automatic thinking that happens and stopping this eliminates the negative effect on the body/mind. It is still a work in progress but has made all the difference to the quality of my life.

Learning how the limbic system/brain would override postural changes influenced how I worked with clients. Slowly strengthening the awareness of the body and changing the unconscious thinking and movement patterns allowed clients to integrate and support the wholeness they were seeking. Learning to think and move with a deeper conscious understanding, brings to and gives one a greater sense of presence and being in the moment.

I still think of the body as an archaeological site, a place where memories and experiences are stored. Memories, even unconscious ones, will carry physical responses or reactions. Unwinding this gives my clients a greater ability to be fully present and more in touch with ease and pleasure. The body is also the temple of God/Goddess, and when treated as such the heart opens and we can connect to the world in a loving way.

Noticing my body and posture gave me insight to my reactions and how easily they could go out of control. This understanding allowed me to stay calmer, no matter what was going on around me. I was no longer triggered by my past, reacting to historical baggage.

These days, I no longer get so sick or became easily upset. I feel fortunate to have found myself on this path to peace and alignment within myself. Following this path and trusting is an ongoing process. Embracing the walls that seem to pop up rather than resist them has helped me find pleasure and gives a sense of centering my body. Sharing this process, and my awareness of the conscious role the body plays in our self-actualization, has become my mission.

ABOUT THE AUTHOR: For over thirty years Elaine has been helping people understand their bodies, get out of pain, and live authentic lives. After receiving her B.A. in Education, Elaine taught school in Los Angeles before moving to San Francisco to study Postural Integration with Jack Painter. Elaine worked as a body therapist for seven years before beginning her training in the Alexander Institute, also located in San Francisco. In 1984 she completed the three-year program and became a certified instructor. She also studied Reichian Therapy with Dr. Peter Levine, Body-Mind Centering with Bonnie Bainbridge-Cohen, and Transpersonal Body Therapy with the Hendricks.

Elaine Belle
elainebelle.com
mimilabelle@comcast.net
415-948-8523

Full Circle to Self-love
Melanie Channell

When I was a young girl, I remember knowing when events were going to happen; I was also very sensitive to other people's feelings. When these incidents occurred I would, like most children, go tell my mother. Time and time again, she would dismiss my accounts, telling me they were just my overactive imagination and eventually tearing down my belief in my spiritual gifts. This invalidation was typical in a family such as mine, where children were generally seen and not heard and girls were considered second-class citizens.

The religion I was raised in was governed by men and all spiritual authority was placed in their hands. My stepfather was a devout follower who forced me to wear homemade, outdated dresses that reached past my knees; I certainly wasn't allowed to wear makeup. It was the early seventies, when short skirts, hot pants, and painted faces were the in thing. Tall, gangly, and awkward, I could feel the eyes of my peers following me as I slunk by in my strange garb. Their laughter, and the feelings of rejection it brought about, left me extremely sensitive and painfully shy.

As an adolescent l fell in with the unruly crowd, so my stepdad transferred me to the high school where he taught English. This did little to control my behavior, however, as I soon aligned myself with the partiers that congregated in the parking lot. I numbed-out the pain of an inferiority complex and abandonment issues stemming from my parent's divorce when I was two, followed by a traumatic move from Washington to California with my mother and her new husband. These events, coupled with the feelings of rejection by my father, led me to make frequent foolish decisions, including running around with depraved men, drug and alcohol abuse, and eventually getting expelled from school. At one point, my parents and even some of my girlfriends thought I had gone mad.

I wasn't really drawn to office work, but my mother steered me in that direction because it was what she knew and she was fed up with my shenanigans. She was a secretary and very good at it, while I was mediocre at best. I worked a few low-paying, dead-end jobs hoping to find my niche. I always wound up in the background, the quiet little mouse who was afraid of her own shadow and became the office doormat for fear of being fired.

I often wondered why my mother didn't prepare me for the psychological landscape of the corporate environment of the early eighties. One boss asked me to go to Lake Tahoe for the weekend and when I said no, he sent me packing. At another job I was tied to the phone and wasn't even allowed to go to the restroom except at break time. The fear of being fired always seemed to be looming over me. I never felt like I was good enough in any of the office jobs I held.

Around this time I met a handsome young artist who lived across the street. We fell head over heels in love, and after dating for a while we moved in together and eventually married. He crafted and sold wooden toys at craft shows for a living, and we traveled all over California. We had a lot of fun camping, saw some beautiful sites, and made new friends who followed the craft circuit. We both liked to drink and smoke cigarettes. Most of the time the drinking was enjoyable, but there were also some terrible fights when we got a little too "lit."

In my early thirties, I returned to corporate life as the project manager at an insurance company. One of my responsibilities was to track every project I was involved with and jot down how long each task took. I had a coworker who made a lot of mistakes because she worked so fast. I had to correct a lot of her errors, but because she completed her tasks so quickly she got a higher pay raise than me. They also gave employees bad marks for taking sick days. Almost half the people in that company were taking antidepressants for stress. After three and a half years there I got ill and had to take a leave of absence. Shortly after that the company started laying people off; I was let go during the second round.

By then I had been sober for a couple of years, but my husband was still drinking heavily, which led to frequent arguments and sometimes vicious fights. Believing he had a serious problem, I started attending Al-Anon meetings to get the support I needed. When he started stashing booze in various hiding places around the house, I gave him an ultimatum. He assured me he was going to AA when he was really going to the bar. We divorced when I was thirty-eight.

During the months that followed, I was feeling rather desperate and alone. One day when I was feeling especially anxious, I passed a psychic gift shop and decided to stop and see what it was all about. The religion that I grew up in taught that it was a sin to go to psychics so I was petrified, but that day I had my first reading. Later that month I had my first energy healing. I literally felt like a different person—cool, calm, and collected. That was the beginning of my journey to self-discovery and my spiritual gifts.

I kept going back to different psychics, primarily to see if and when I would find true love again. I met with a woman who told me not to look for a mate, because I would meet someone special in about six months—a man with reddish-brown hair and a mustache, and who worked with his hands. I pictured this man in meditation one night so I knew precisely what he looked like, but I never could have imagined how we would meet. My ex-husband had met a woman who accidentally dialed the wrong number one evening, and after they moved in together she introduced me by phone to her ex-boyfriend. A couple of weeks later he and I met at Denny's. I immediately knew this was divine intervention—he was the same man the psychic had told me about six months earlier and who I had envisioned in meditation! We were married six months later.

The next job I accepted was in the accounting department of yet another construction company. The co-owners of this company were polar opposites: one was happy-go-lucky and the other was a bona fide narcissist. I intensely disliked working for the narcissist, who loved to yell at and embarrass people. He would give me an assignment and direct me to do it exactly how he instructed—no questions asked—yet I always had to deal with numerous mistakes and several modifications. I didn't know it at the time, but I had been guided to take this particular job for a specific reason.

The owners had connections with a three-day leadership training program and would send employees who wanted to participate to the seminar. When I was invited, previous participants wouldn't divulge anything about their experience so I was nervous. I was still quite reserved, so for me it was a real leap of faith to attend. The experiences I had in those three difficult yet enlightening days were literally life-changing. My grandmother came through one woman and I saw a spirit guide standing behind another. It's like a light switch turned on inside me. I walked out of that training with my heart singing. I had discovered my life purpose and my passion for healing.

I was already a Reiki Master but suddenly I wanted more. I started taking more energy healing classes at night, got certified in spiritual counseling, and poured my heart and soul into learning everything I could about metaphysics and spiritual concepts. I was guided to start a metaphysical Meetup group to learn how to speak in front of people. I had discovered in the leadership training that getting out of my comfort zone would support my growth. A friend told me to feel the fear and do it anyway.

I eventually was guided to learn about and work with angels and started teaching angel classes. During this time, I started having more spiritual experiences, seeing auras, and seeing, smelling, and hearing spirits. I sometimes smelled gardenias which were my grandmother's favorite flower, and my grandfather's pipe smoke would permeate the air. When my cat passed away, I saw her running up the walkway for about a week after she was gone.

Then the unexpected happened. In October of 2008, my husband was told his kidneys weren't functioning well and he was going to need dialysis. This news came in during the Great Recession, and by May of 2009 my hours at work had dwindled down to three days a week. I was laid off right before my husband, who had been getting progressively weaker, was put on dialysis.

I saw being unemployed as an opportunity to assist my ailing husband and also to create a spiritual healing business. I started reading tarot cards, writing more spiritual classes, and even produced a few Healing Expos with a friend.

When the time came for me to find work again, I put an ad online for a part-time job so that I could continue growing my business and be available for my husband if he needed me. Within two weeks, the perfect opportunity came along. It was a part-time position that was very flexible and would allow me the time off I needed.

Since then, I have been working on growing my spiritual business by participating in psychic and healing fairs, teaching classes, and learning and working with new technology as it presents itself. I am very grateful to God and all the earth angels that have shared their love and spiritual tools to assist me through this journey called life.

When we come into this world, we bring with us special gifts and talents born out of love. Our heart and soul are connected to these abilities and yearn to develop these gifts to share with the world. Some of us tap right in to our abilities and continue to polish them throughout our lives, but many of us follow other people's ideas of what is best for us and delay or never live our true heart's desire. I was one who took the long way around, but when the call finally came I picked up the phone.

ABOUT THE AUTHOR: Melanie Channell is a certified spiritual counselor/tarot reader, Numerologist, Chios Master Teacher, crystal healer, and angel enthusiast. She has been certified in over sixty energy healing modalities and has been studying spirituality and empowerment concepts for over twenty years. Melanie finds joy in helping people clear out old energy patterns and learning to take responsibility for their own healing process. She is passionate about empowering people to make choices that will steer them toward their life purpose and personal happiness. Melanie enjoys participating as a vendor and speaking at psychic fairs to help spread positivity and healing throughout northern California.

Melanie Channell
Heart Works
heartworksnow.com
Melanie_Channell@yahoo.com
916-920-7832

Hope, Healthy, and Happiness
Peggy Yu

I should have died twenty years ago. After years of severe depression, anxiety, panic attacks, and an eating disorder, I tried to commit suicide. I could no longer take the pain of the childhood sexual molestation I had endured, along with the physical, emotional, and verbal abuse by my parents, and a body damaged from overuse of a steroid for my childhood asthma. But something in me kept searching for the answers, and I finally found hope, health, and true happiness. I am just a regular human being, so if I can survive and thrive, anyone can.

I was the first child, followed by three sisters. At age three, I had a terrible cold which turned to bronchitis and, later, chronic asthma. Every time the weather was cold and damp, I struggled for breath. The whizzing sound of my breathing disturbed everyone in the family, and it got even worse at night. My father would hear my uncontrollable coughing and yell at me in disgust. "Be brave, don't behave like a wimp!! Stop the cough!" I thought, they surely cannot feel my pain, otherwise they wouldn't be so cold-hearted, so annoyed by my cough. My parents were only in their mid-twenties and struggling financially. They had both come from big families—mom had nine siblings, dad had seven—and both had lost parents at a very young age and had suffered financially as a result. However, as a kid, I did not understand their hardships; I just knew they cared only about the money and not about me. I felt very sad and alone.

My parents always told that as the oldest, it was my responsibility to take care and to protect my sisters. I took that into my heart; it was up to me to prevent my sisters from harm. One day, a teenage cousin arrived at our home. He was going to work for my parents and babysit us if they were too busy. I thought it was nice to have someone older look after us, but I was being naïve. One sunny summer afternoon, while my parents were out running errands that cousin tried to do something strange to us. Just eight years old, I was not sure what he was doing but I could sense the danger. I quickly locked my younger sisters in the truck and told them we were playing a game. He molested me and threatened me not to tell my parents. I did not tell them, or anyone else but I did not feel right. I felt invaded. My only consolation was that I had protected my sisters from harm.

Every winter I got asthma attacks. Though I was still young, I would have to go to the emergency room by myself and get the "magic shot," the steroid. Little did my parents and I know that chronic use of this steroid would cause a lot of problems down the road. According to American Addiction Centers (2016), long-term use of steroids may cause fertility issues, rapid mood swings and menstrual irregularities. It wasn't until after I learned Traditional Chinese Medicine a couple years ago that I realized there is more than one kind of asthma, each with a different cause and different treatments. Mostly, asthma is caused by weakness in the lungs, however, a weak digestive system or kidney function can also contribute to shortness of breath, low energy, low voice, spontaneous sweating, palpitation, pale skin, poor appetite, depression, sadness, and fatigue. When the kidneys are involved there may also be difficulty lying flat, swollen lymph nodes, palpitations, feelings of fear, urinary issues, and cold limbs.

As I mentioned, my parents and I knew nothing of these and besides, the steroid shot was the only way to save my life. It would turn out to be a quick fix that would cause me huge problems down the road.

Side effects from the steroids, coupled with the sexual molestation, I was always concerned about my appearance. I was chubby and had bigger breasts than other girls my age. I also began menstruating at a very early age. People described me as a happy girl with big smile on my face but deep down there was a big dark hole in my heart.

One day in the third grade, a teacher from the next class stopped me in the hallway and pretended to check the stack of classroom assignments that I was holding with my hands. Suddenly, he started to rub against my breast! The memories from the childhood molestation instantly came rushing back; a chill ran up my back and I could even smell the same body odor from my cousin. I felt ill and nauseous on my way home, and when my parents asked me what was wrong I told them what happened in school and, finally, what the cousin had done to me. They were shocked, but did nothing to stand up for me or protect me. The mother of the cousin had lent them money for their business, and they did not want to lose face in my school. This betrayal traumatized me more than the molestation and led to ten years of resentment and hatred for my parents. Despite my broken heart I continued to get good grades, knowing I had to to get a good job in the future. I did not want to rely on them. We never fought, but I lived in a constant state of hypervigilance with high levels of cortisol, and suppressing my true feelings. I ignored them, hoping that one day it would get better, but the pain of it all continued to wear on me.

One day, I tried to commit suicide. Even now, I can still see the blood stain on my mattress. My mother was sad and asked why I was so silly. I told her I was not well but she did not know how to help. There was no proper education or resources around mental illness in Asia back then. Thinking I was possessed by something evil, she took me to a temple and asked the monks to expel it. Of course, it did not work for me. The cause was not evil, but the trauma and lack of support from them. But I forced myself to keep going and suppressed the feelings.

There was one adult who was always there for me—my aunt. Kind and caring, she often looked after me when my parents were too busy. Then, early one August morning when I was in the tenth grade, the family was awoken by the sharp ringing of the phone. My aunt had hung herself. I was stunned and speechless. We had just talked to each other the day before on my way home from school. She was smiling and encouraged me to keep up my good grades. What had happened since then? I knew she suffered from terrible lower back pain because of a car accident, but she was a nurse—she should know it would take time to heal, so why? No one had any answers for me. I lost the only person that I trusted. Not knowing what else to do I suppressed more, and drew further inward. The distance between myself and parents grew wider as well.

Over time, I developed self-destructive behaviors to numb the pain. I was never drawn to illegal substances; instead, I would binge eat and then make myself vomit. I also shopped like crazy, which gave me a reason to work even harder to pay the bill and to feel that I was still alive. After vomiting, I would have terrible panic attacks and felt my heart was going to jump out of my throat. I developed terrible depression as well. When I told my mom that I was not feeling well physically and mentally, she said I was just being lazy and that I was a big fat ass. They often compared me with other kids in the neighborhood and found me lacking. When I did something wrong, they would lift me up like a little dog and whip me with metal hangers or a belt. It took days for the bruises to go away. This was a common practice in Asia at that time, and there were no social workers or child protective services. I was not the only child being treated like that. And still, I kept going, numbed.

I met my ex-husband online. This was seventeen years ago, when online dating was still relatively rare. What started out as language practice turned into chatting about other things. Two years later, we were married. He was much older than me, and I thought I had finally found the security I longed for. I was wrong. Though he was nice and caring and provided a means of escape from my suffocating environment, he held the same beliefs that a woman should not have a voice. Instead, we should be satisfied with a roof above your head and food to eat every day. He couldn't understand how I needed to heal from my pain.

My miscarriage was the turning point. It was the only chance to have a child of my own. His lack of support during this terrible time woke me up completely. I left him and worked hard to find myself. I was tired of being tired, weak, hopeless, and unhappy. I knew there had to be answers for all my questions.

I went back to school and got my master's degree in counselling psychology. I began to understand the connection between childhood sexual trauma, the response from caregivers, long-term distress, and the imbalance in mind and body. This imbalance often causes depression, anxiety, and even irregular menstruation and infertility due to early exposure to sexual touch. My mentor, Lesley, applied TIR (Traumatic Incident Reduction) to help me deal with my first trauma. This was followed by DBT (Dialectic Behaviour Therapy) training, where I learned to apply skills I learned—such as mindfulness, the five-senses method, and being non-judgmental, yet I still felt something was missing. I still didn't feel well physically, so I started fitness and nutritional training with my coach, Steve.

Later, while in the San Francisco area, I found NET (Neuro Emotional Technique); this technique works on the feelings and emotions that are trapped in our nerves as memories. From there I trained in the four-thousand-year-old study of the connection between emotions and specific meridians in the body, i.e. anger to liver, joy to heart, fear to kidneys, sadness to lungs, and low self-esteem to the digestive system. Slowly but sure I began removing and adjusting the blocks in my body.

Layer after painful layer, I uncovered the correlation between mind and illness. By shedding each unwanted feeling, my mind became lighter and my body healthier. Now I do not have to pretend to be happy because it comes from within. There is no more clown mask that I used to wear when I was young. I finally understand and realize that mind and body is a holistic organism. When there is pain in body, the brain sends a signal to the person, to warn. When there is a pain in mind, the mind also sends a signal to inform you in the form of feelings. There are no right or wrong feelings; having a neutral stance is the key for living a balanced life. No one could tell me to forgive my parents or forget about what happened—I had to decide myself to let go of the pain. Now I understand that they also had their struggles and were trying to get through their own pain, and I appreciate that they pushed me to be independent and fight for myself. I can even remember the happy times with them.

The human body has a tremendous ability to heal; there is always a cure for every wound. There is also always a way to find hope, health, and happiness. After almost two decades, I found it, and I am sure you can too.

ABOUT THE AUTHOR: Peggy Yu is a Registered Clinical Counsellor and a Registered Acupuncturist who has dedicated her life to helping people. She has held various positions in programs funded by the Canadian government, including as a liaison for immigrant settlement programs, a family therapist, and as an Addiction Clinical Counsellor. She has also volunteered as a Victim Services Support Worker for at the local police department. Peggy's work is based in the mind-body connection, the inherent neutrality of emotions, and that it is always better to treat the root cause rather than just the symptoms. In her free time, Peggy enjoys hiking with her therapy dog, Smokey.

Peggy Yu
PH7 Mind and Body Wellness
ph7mindnbody.com
peggyyu@shaw.ca
604-807-9680

From Pain to Passion
Jennifer Nolan

We each have a story, with its unique experiences, perspectives, and timeline. These experiences in turn create thoughts and beliefs which then shape our futures. Though I didn't know it at the time, my story, which was rooted in a dysfunctional family, would be a driving factor in the passion, purpose, and plan for my life.

My mom was in her twenties when she was diagnosed with schizophrenia. Though just a child, I had already observed unusual behaviors that were difficult to process, and would remain so throughout my teenage years and into young adulthood. Most days I woke up uncertain and fearful about what her mood would be. This led to a lot of embarrassing situations, particularly during my middle school and high school years, when I was trying to navigate the changes of adolescence. Being around others was uncomfortable, for I never knew what my mom would say or do. I felt she loved me but didn't understand me, and I certainly didn't understand her. I pulled away from her, spending most of my time out of the house or holed up in my room. When we were together, my mom and I had a lot of shouting matches, often punctuated with slamming doors. Looking back, I realize I was angry at her for not being what I thought she should be, and for not providing me with the safe place, communication, and relationship other girls had with their mothers. In fact, my friends told me more than once that they would run away if they had to deal with what I did.

Like most teens I fought for independence; part of me however, began to take on the role of "parent"; I was under the assumption that I needed to be responsible for others' well-being, that I couldn't be okay or at peace if those around me were not. Manipulation and stubbornness were tools that I used to control the unexpected and confusing situations around me.

My father did everything he could to provide me and my brother with a stable home life. He was always telling us he loved us, and he prioritized spending time with us over money, success, and personal hobbies. He also took the time to do with us things he knew we were interested in. Most importantly, he provided me with an invaluable example of perseverance in the midst of painful uncertainty. I watched as he faithfully and continually prayed, read books, and tried many different options/ways in the hopes of helping my mom. I remember how he helped others financially and spiritually. People loved being around him because he was a good listener and truly showed interest in their lives.

I too prayed a lot while growing up. Two specific requests I remember making were for wisdom and a husband, and, at the age of twenty, I was blessed to marry my childhood sweetheart. I deeply desired and fervently prayed for God to show me how to have a healthy, happy, and authentic relationship with my husband and with our future children.

This yearning led me to read every book about family, marriage, and parenting that I could get my hands on. I also paid close attention to how other families interacted with each other. Basically, I thought that by immersing myself in all things "family" I would have insight and understanding into what I wanted my own family life to look like.

Over the years being a wife and a mother always remained my primary focus and priority. Like every family we had our ups and downs, but any sacrifices my husband and I made were well worth it, for our children were happy, healthy, and well adjusted. God had indeed blessed us many times over.

In 2014, my settled, comfortable existence was shaken when

my mother was moved to our area. For the first time in about twenty years, I was confronted with the responsibility of engaging with her.

I reluctantly decided to call her once a week because I thought it was the right thing to do, but the calls always ended in arguments and hurt feelings.

I had no idea how to make things better, and the resulting frustration affected every aspect of my life. My husband was getting the worst of me and not the best of me. I came to realize that my behavior was rooted in the false beliefs I had brought into my marriage and had never come to terms with. Knowing I had to let go of this way of thinking, I prayed to know how my Heavenly Father wanted me to handle it.

As always, God came through, by placing key people and opportunities in my path that helped me find clarity and life direction. In 2015, I enrolled in the Institute for Professional Excellence in Coaching to become a Certified Life Coach. It's here that I learned every aspect of creating a partnership to help others better manage their lives, create greater fulfillment, and identify and live their dreams. This training opened my eyes to the importance of self-awareness and how to be a better listener and communicator. As you can imagine, it positively impacted my relationship with my husband and teenagers.

This led me to pursue training at my church to become a spiritual mentor. I worked with women in all different stages of life to help them identify any defeating patterns of thinking/behaving that had caused them to be stuck; recognize the false beliefs that developed during their formative years and were affecting their adult relationships; and finally, to show them how to replace those false beliefs with truths, thereby freeing them to walk in their God-given identity. As with my life coaching training, these lessons also helped me understand my own history and the ways in which it had held me captive.

One of the turning points in my transformation came as a result of exploring the work of Drs. Caroline Leaf and Peter Breggin. Leaf, a neuroscientist, had spent twenty-five years researching the mind-body connection as it relates to thinking, learning, feeling, and healing from traumatic brain injury (TBI) and other neurological issues. Her wisdom helped me recognize the power of my thoughts and the way they affected my responses to everything in my life. Dr. Breggin, M.D., is one of the world's foremost critics of biological psychiatry and a staunch advocate for psychological and social human services. His work both brought me profound insights about the mind and brain functionality, specifically how they are affected by antipsychotic medications, which tremendously helped me understand my mom's mental struggles.

During this time of discovery, understanding truths, and taking control of my thoughts, I found "calm in the chaos." I found "clarity in the midst of the uncertainty."

For the first time, I realized that my mother had no control over certain areas of her life. Her authentic self was "masked" by the emotions and suppressed pain and trauma from her past, and from forty years of taking toxic medications. In other words, she had been living like a prisoner in her own mind and didn't know how to get out. When she hurt others, she was actually acting from her own pain.

These realizations helped me to understand my mother—and love her—in a way I never had before.

This quote by Thomas Merton sums it up perfectly: "The beginning of love is to let those we love be perfectly themselves, and not to twist them to fit our own image. Otherwise we love only the reflection of ourselves we find in them."

Through this long but necessary and powerful process, God

brought healing and transformation to my thought life. My mom and I now have conversations; we laugh and share time together. We have the happy, healthy, and real "relationship" I so longed for as a child. Currently, my brother and I are intentionally working together with our mom to help her find clarity with the personal and psychological issues in her life and to help her live out the remainder of her life with the freedom to be happy, healthy, and her authentic self.

Today, my mom is my hero. My biggest prayer warrior. She's one of the most generous and compassionate people I know, a woman, who, despite the mental suffering and being misunderstood for much of her life, has chosen to remain faithful to her Heavenly Father and to her family.

Today, I am grateful and blessed to enjoy happy, healthy, and authentic relationships with Michael, my best friend and husband of twenty-three years; my nineteen-year-old son Wesley; and my sixteen-year-old daughter, Madyson.

Most incredibly, God has taken my past pain and turned it into my life's passion—a passion to help hurting families find healing and restoration in their struggling relationships. My past confusion has become my purpose—a purpose to partner with those who have lost their identity along the way and want to walk in power, in love, and with a sound mind every day. My broken story has become God's plan for my life. A plan to connect family members where each person is allowed the freedom for independence to contribute their own unique gifts, perspectives, and work together as a team.

We each have a unique and powerful journey that "no one else" can live. If we will choose to discover our unique blueprint, embrace the truths that set us free, and renew our mind every day, we will live in our authentic self. We will find the passion, purpose, and plan God has for us. We will find what has been sleeping deep inside of our being waiting to be brought to life. As Jennie Allen says so well in her devotional, "Discover God's Dream for You," "What if the greatest thing you have to give the world is hidden in your darkest moments? What if your scars point to a greater story?"

ABOUT THE AUTHOR: Jennifer Nolan is a Professional Certified Life Coach known for her open mind, empathetic listening skills, and a passion for connecting with young adults to help them discover and create their own authentic and powerful journeys. She serves at her church in the High School Ministry program, where for the past six years she has been leading, mentoring, and living "Life" with a large group of remarkable young ladies. Jennifer also volunteers in the Care Ministry program, helping women of various ages explore the connection between their beliefs about themselves and their quality of life. She is currently working on her first book entitled, "Your Powerful Journey."

Jennifer Nolan, Certified Professional Mentor Coach
Your Powerful Journey - Explore. Embrace. Empower.
jennifernolan702@gmail.com
jennifernolan.org
770-366-9494

No One Is You …
That Is Your Superpower!
Rae Roach

Just be you. At one point or another, most of us have gotten this advice, from a parent, teacher, or friend. But what does that mean? I certainly did not know; in fact I had been trying to get back to "me" my entire life. The problem was, I didn't even know who "me" was. No matter where I was, I felt I didn't belong, and over time, I had gotten used to having a mask on for every situation and every person I was around.

It would take fifty-eight years and a lot of pain before I was finally able to take the masks off and come to terms with EVERYthing!! Some might say, good grief, Rae, fifty-eight years—what took so long? What they don't realize is that every bad decision, wrong turn, failed relationship, career change, financial ruin—even when my life completely fell apart—has led me to ME. And for that I am forever grateful. I am also grateful for everyone who has been there throughout my journey, whether you remained solid with me or dropped off along the way. No matter what your role was, I could not have done it without you. We all have a backstory, and as a friend of mine says, those are just the facts—if you aren't happy with your life then just rewrite your story. Here's mine: At a very early age, I knew I was different from my family. I honestly thought I must've been switched at birth and dreamt of the day my "real" family would come for me (when I finally told my mom this just a few years ago, she replied, "So did I, at times.") There was absolutely nothing wrong with my family,

I just wanted more. I wanted to experience the world. I wanted acclaim … I wanted status … I wanted to be KNOWN!

By my mid-thirties I thought I had reached my "goal." I had a great career, a doting husband, two handsome, intelligent boys, a beautifully decorated home, cleaning service, exotic vacations, designer clothes, monthly massages, manicure/pedicures, and perfectly coiffed hair. I had arrived! But wait—had I? I still found myself searching; I still had that sense that I was just drifting through life. Despite the fact I was SURE I had direction and a path to follow, I would get bored and anxious; I kept switching from career to career, each time with serious doubts as to whether I had ever made the right decision or done the right thing.

Why? Why wasn't I happy?

Because despite my many changes, I still wasn't living my life's purpose. I was living in what the Toltec's call The Dream of The Planet. I was living society's reality rather than my own. In his usual simple yet deeply profound manner, Wayne Dyer had said, "If you change the way you look at things, the things you look at change." I was still wondering precisely how to do this when the Universe showed me the way … the *hard way*…

Underneath the perfect façade, my world—and my marriage—was crumbling. After a divorce that devastated me financially, emotionally, mentally, and spiritually, I found myself left to raise my two young boys alone. That's when it really hit me: I had absolutely NO idea who I was. Eventually, I would realize that I had always been lost; the self-assured, in-control person I presented to the world was an illusion. Internally, I was a mess!

During this time I wasn't able to do the simplest of things, the things that I was known to be a BEAST with; organizing, putting things together, list-making, multitasking, Queen of Getting Shit Done! Now they were too much to handle. Once I let the emotional toll of the events control me, the true spiral downward began. I hit rock bottom—gaining about fifty pounds and, due to my inability to function, going through my savings and retirement money. My house was even foreclosed on, leaving me with nowhere to live. But the beauty of being at the bottom is the only direction you can go is UP.

Journey to Me

Just because there is one way to go does not mean the path is easy, however. As I struggled I started rebuilding my spirit and soul and that's when I discovered my purpose and passion—to give back and assist others in finding their true authentic self. I truly believe I have a voice and a message that will help, guide, inspire, and motivate other women (and men too!) to stay true to themselves while navigating the roadblocks life throws at us. And trust me, these roadblocks and self-discovery can be extremely painful. I will tell you there were many, many times I wanted to give up, quit trying, and just wallow in my self-deprecating thoughts. Better the devil you know than the one you don't, right??

I began to understand that when we tap into our heart space we make it possible for our truth to immerge, for our innate wisdom and our intuition to awaken. We make it possible for spirit to be heard.

I exposed a nerve when I tried to connect with my heart center. It felt unnatural and dark—the place where fear resides. Why? It was a place that was unfamiliar to me, yet somehow I knew if I was ever going to expand, if I was ever going to truly live, I had to embrace not only my fears, but my insecurities and vulnerabilities as well.

In my self-work I have been studying many individuals in the fields of self-development and spiritual growth. The ones I gravitate towards are Wayne Dyer, Don Miguel Ruiz, Sr. and Jr., Don Jose Ruiz, Susan Jeffers, and the teachings of Abraham. Some of the things I have gleaned from these individuals were life-changing; feel the fear and do it anyway; stay in "your vortex," you can't solve the problem with the same mind that created it; you can only control to the tip of your finger; live authentically; don't take things personally; your opinion of ME is none of MY business (sit with that one for a minute!); give up your personal history, and don't die with the music still in you. These are just a few thoughts that I now live by but more importantly, I have learned to embrace silence.

Among these teachings there are three that truly changed my life and the way I looked at things:

1. Ho'oponopono. I realized that I *had* to reconcile and release each hurtful relationship and memory. This was DEEP! How could I do that? There is a quote that says; "I never knew how strong I was until I had to forgive someone who wasn't sorry, and accept an apology I never received." Yea—that ain't gonna happen!! What helped me through this process was the Hawaiian Forgiveness Prayer, Ho'oponopono. With each hurtful relationship and memory I said this prayer until I was finally able to stop the bawling. This took months, but afterwards I was finally able to look at memories through a different lens, and with a vastly different emotional reaction.

   When I did the prayer I didn't direct it towards my "tormentor" because I firmly believe I am not the one that needs to forgive them, rather, I needed to forgive myself for the part I played, the thoughts I had surrounding it, the emotions I felt because of it, and the blame I placed on others that really belonged to me.

   It is a four-part, seemingly simple, prayer that delivers profound results:

   1) I'm Sorry (Repentance)
   2) Please Forgive Me (Forgiveness)
   3) Thank You (Gratitude)

       4) I Love You (Love)
2. The Four Agreements by Don Miguel Ruiz. This tiny little book has four agreements with yourself that seemed simple yet were incredibly hard to implement. But as I started understanding and living by the Four Agreements my heart and my soul began to merge.

       1) Be Impeccable With Your Word
       2) Don't Take Anything Personally (my biggest challenge!)
       3) Don't Make Assumptions
       4) Always Do Your Best

3. Trust the Process. Along the way it became apparent to me the process in healing each and every wound, eliminating those self-limiting beliefs, learning to love ME as I am, releasing my attachments and judgments was the same.

Sit with it—allow it—learn from it—grow because of it. Instead of pushing it back down, ignoring it, and smiling through it, I had to sit with the feeling/emotion no matter how uncomfortable, no matter how long. I had to allow the emotion/feeling to run its course, no matter how painful. And when I did that I was able to see the lesson it was to teach me. And from there was able to grow because of it!

I attended a workshop where we were asked, "What fear do you feel is holding you back?" I was the last to respond, and as each participant talked about his/her fears I felt a connection with each but had a serious revelation—I no longer felt the fear of them. Now, let me be completely honest here, just because I no longer felt the fear does NOT mean I no longer feel fearful. I do! But I realized that I no longer felt the crippling/paralyzing effects of that fear.

This was a MAJOR breakthrough for me because I had lived most of my life in fear: fear of the unknown, fear of not having control, fear of what people thought of me, my decisions, the direction I truly wanted to go, fear that no one would accept me AS ME, and the biggest fear of all—that I am unlovable. And those were just a few! How did these fears abate, you might ask? Well, it took years of self-work, much of which was excruciatingly painful. It is only now, as I sit on the other side of it, that I look back and see the craziness of it all. We all think we are protecting ourselves by staying in our "comfort zones," or by ignoring the problem/situation, or swallowing the pain, hurt, guilt, shame, regret—you name it. But in truth, I never understood how confining my comfort zone was until I finally stepped out of it.

Here's my re-write: I am learning to let the concept of time go and stop questioning the Divine Universe's timeline for me. Letting go and acceptance is a journey, a journey that continues each and every day. I have always believed in the holistic approach. However, it wasn't until I began the journey of self-discovery—first by eliminating the negative energy around me and then by surrounding myself with women whose sole interest was to encourage, uplift, educate, and empower—did I realize who I really was.

I now stand in my POWER with the knowledge that this life is for the taking. It is mine … it is yours … it is ALL of OURS to take. The Universe is there to deliver to each of us our desires, we just have to realize, accept, and step into it. If we are truly living a heart-centered existence, being our most authentic self—*there is no competition*—I am not taking from you and you are not taking from me!

One of my favorite quotes is by Lily Tomlin: "I always wanted to be someone, I just didn't know who." I felt that statement in the depths of my soul! Now when I think of that quote it brings me such joy. Why, you ask, because I have finally figured out who I want to be… ME!

ABOUT THE AUTHOR: Rae, Founder of Women Helping Women Retreats, has a passion for showing others how to find their voice so they can speak their truth. After a challenging life journey towards finding her own authentic self, Rae is always willing to share her personal struggles and victories, as well as the ways in which she has overcome hurdles to live and enjoy a more peaceful and fulfilling life. A Compassionate Journey Guide, teacher, leader, mentor, and intuitive, Rae can quickly hone in on what is needed to powerfully present a life-changing belief or empowering message. She brings a sincere and understanding voice to her speaking engagements, workshops, seminars, and WHW Retreats.

Rae Roach
Speaker | Visionary
RaeRoachSpeaks@gmail.com
RaeRoach.com
703-200-2110

The Gift of the Lesson
Bonnie Bogner

My belief is that every challenge in life contains an opportunity to learn, grow, explore, and challenge myself in new ways. While we often struggle to find the opportunity hidden amid the chaos, our ability to do so can provide a wealth of peace.

Finding the gift of the lesson takes practice, but it is well worth the effort. This is my story of finding these gifts.

***

I grew up never really feeling like I fit in, aware from an early age that there was much more than meets the eye. I tended to be a loner, preferring the company of nature and animals to that of people. I was very fortunate to have grown up on a farm in rural Saskatchewan, Canada, where I was surrounded by the sanctuary of nature and animals and could just be me.

My early schoolyears were challenging, as I had a difficult time copying notes from the blackboard, spelling, and writing number sequences. Now the condition would be considered dyslexia, at the time, it was just a struggle.

Although at school I felt incompetent that I could not keep up, I was gifted with two loving and understanding parents who guided and assisted me. They never showed any anger or frustration at my inability to do simple tasks, so I knew all was well and I was loved. My parents supported me, no matter what, and my animal friends on the farm did not care if I could spell.

I had no problem thinking or talking about abstract ideas and concrete notions, but I found it difficult to transfer this to paper. I gradually came to realize that I did not see the world in the same way as most, or in the way that was expected in a school environment.

This is still true today; I tend to see things a little differently than most of the people I know. Maybe I can see it more abstractly since it is challenging to put it on paper. I still have a hard time with directions, my spelling is only functional, and the concept of right and left eludes me. My sister lovingly jokes that she is glad she is not in my head, because it is way too busy.

How would my life have been shaped without this challenge? I don't know exactly, only that it would be much different. These experiences have contributed to my ability to apply myself to the task at hand and think outside the box. They have opened me up to acceptance of human differences. I am a more compassionate and accepting person due to my own inability to fit in. This challenge has truly been a blessing on so many levels.

***

My young adult years were spent raising my three amazing, talented, and strong-willed sons and I delved into the journey of single parenthood when they were still very young. Although their father was involved, I was the primary caregiver and most of the parenting tasks fell to me.

The reality was that I could not run my household up to my own standards. I was unable to attend everyone's after school activities, and felt like we were all missing out, but that was our reality. On some of the more hectic days all I could manage was cereal for supper.

I had so many things to be grateful for at that time: I was gainfully employed with flexibility in my schedule; I had a strong support network of family, co-workers, and friends; their dad took them for visits and vacations; I lived within walking distance of their school; and the list goes on.

We lived in a comfortable home and I fulfilled most expectations of what a mother (and father) should provide. I baked and cooked for my family, I worked hard to ensure they had a positive and supportive environment, and I tried to ensure they did not miss out because our family configuration had changed.

When I reflect on those crazy hectic years, it is not the busyness, nor the less than spotless house that I remember. What stands out is how much I love my sons, and how glad I am to have had the privilege of raising them. The love, being together, and finding a way to be happy are far more important than the nutritional value of every meal.

***

In the early nineties I began studying alternative healing, and energy work—with each neuropsychology, energy healing or intuitive development class I took, I told myself this would be The One. I would trust myself and do the work.

After the excitement of each new endeavor wore away, I began looking for the next solution. This went on for many years, with more classes and books than I care to count. That all changed in early 2006 when I decided to not renew my lucrative corporate contract in information technology. Rather I travelled to California to take yet another class, and finally do the work I was called to.

By this time, I was single again, my children were now grown and independent. I had a little money in the bank and a big dream. There was a constant internal nudge to do what I love and do it NOW. My family thought I was crazy, but they supported me, as they always do.

Some days I really felt like I had no idea where I was going or what I was doing. Despite feeing like I was walking into an abyss, I felt compelled to proceed. I told the beings I call my "non-physical team" that I would jump into this work, if they would catch me. In response I felt a vague sense of apprehension and a strong sense of trust. This is what I had come to earth to do, and I knew the time was right to do it.

I think fondly now of those first few Intuitive Readings. I was apprehensive, but there was something much more powerful than my mind pulling me forward into the work. My spirit had a plan, and when I could relax and trust, the plan flowed smoothly.

Many people were having huge and life changing experiences through my private sessions and classes. With each experience my confidence grew, and I believed a little more that I had something worthwhile to offer.

One day as I sat quietly before a client and invited in my non-physical team, I got a surprise. Rather than the usual moment of apprehension that this would be the client I received no insights for, I heard a clear message "You know that you know, and you know that you will always know, now do the work."

That was it! Since then I have always known that each session will be exactly what it is supposed to be. However much, or little, guidance I receive, it is exactly right for that client. I do indeed "know that I know."

Once I was able to surrender my need to control the process and simply be in the moment and receive appropriate guidance, I was able to trust my non-physical team.

***

Over years of working with clients, I came to realize that most were looking for a specific outcome; they wanted to achieve a certain goal to be happy. However, these achievements are fleeting; as soon as one goal is reached, we start looking for the next one. What if we could simply love the process rather than need to arrive somewhere to be happy?

When I finally took the leap from corporate employment to self-responsible independent, I thought I had found IT—now I could be happy. I was following my passion, tapping into my intuition, and helping people. However, that was just the beginning, for we are all in a constant state of impermanence and I continued to grow and evolve. I have learned to surrender to most of what Spirit asks of me and simply be in the flow. In this state of flow, I find I am able to let go of judgement and be more fully in observation.

We most often start our observation process in judgement, deciding if we like or dislike something. It is simply how we operate. The magic happens if we can go to the next step and let go of our preferences in favor of observation and wondering. "Wondering" about what you are experiencing can bring you into a state of grace, which in turn allows you to be more present in the flow, rather than attempting to control it and direct it towards your preferences.

***

I had been working for several years as a Spiritual Coach and Intuitive, breaking trail for those who believed in Angels and knew there was "something more". I was content and on purpose with what I was doing until an event occurred that would forever change my life.

I was facilitating a solstice celebration and we were well into the meditation when I saw a group of very tall, slender, non-physical beings walk into the room. Please understand, I am primarily claircognizant, which means I internally *know* things rather than seeing visions, but I clearly saw these beings! They had an air of peace and benevolence and they spoke clearly to me, although there was no sound. They indicated they were there to do a DNA Activation, and I wondered what that was, and what it had to do with me.

Their response was that they must transmit through someone in physical form, and I was to get the group's consent to receive this energy, as they never transmitted without permission. Feeling a bit like a fraud, I asked the group to give their permission to receive a very special energy transmission. As I paused for the group to absorb what was about to happen, I saw a being step behind each one of the meditators and place their hands over the persons head. I was astonished to see the most amazing iridescent rainbow colors and sacred geometric shapes pour out of their hands.

I have no idea how long that meditation lasted, or how long the beings continued to transmit this energy to the group; it seemed timeless. When this was done, the group was particularly radiant and content. After the event was over, one of the participants came to me and asked who the tall beings were who had been in the room with us!

Thus, began my beautiful relationship with a group of ascended beings who I have come to know as the Galactic Council. It continues to be a journey of frustration and fun, doubt and trust, as we work together, and I come to know them. They have been patient but persistent teachers as I navigate gingerly through the relatively uncharted world of channelling.

One of my biggest challenges is to allow my voice to be heard in this non-conventional way, yet it is also a gift to be able to share their wisdom with family, friends, and clients. As I have found my own voice as a channel, I have become more confident and willing to share the messages.

From this unique relationship I have learned to be in the center of my own orbit and allow others to have their opinions of me and what I do. Whenever we let another's opinion matter more than our own, we give away our power. What others think of us actually has very little to do with us and far more to do with them. Only our reaction has to do with us. This is not always easy for me to accept, but it is getting easier all the time, and I know all the other lessons in my life were preparing me specifically for my purpose. When you can truly understand the benefits of a challenge in your life, it no longer needs to be a challenge—it can then become a

lesson, and maybe even a gift.

ABOUT THE AUTHOR: Bonnie Bogner possesses a passion and curiosity about all things metaphysical and has spent many years studying spirituality and healing modalities such as NLP, Spiritual Coaching, Hawaiian Healing, and Angels. Several years ago, the Galactic Council made their presence known to her and became her multidimensional guides. Their wisdom and teaching now blend with all her studies to create the Soul Alignment process. Bonnie lives her life as a role model and beacon of light for those who are searching for a heart-centered and spiritually-directed experience. Bonnie offers private coaching and channelling sessions and workshops, as well as spiritual retreats around the world.

Bonnie Bogner
Soul Alignment Coach & Ambassador of Galactic Wisdom
soulvibrations.ca
bonnie@soulvibrations.ca
facebook.com/groups/gcwisdom

Fourteen Days of Zen & Writing in France with Natalie Goldberg

Anneli Davey

"The most regretful people on earth are those who felt the call to creative work, who felt their own creative power restive and uprising, and gave to it neither power nor time." ~ Mary Oliver, poet

In the autumn of 2014, in my 50th year, I traveled from my cottage on Vancouver Island, British Columbia, to France for *The True Secret of Writing*, a two-week silent retreat with the beloved Zen and writing teacher, Natalie Goldberg.

The retreat changed the way I live my life.

The bus winds through the French countryside from the train station to the Ferme de Villefavard, an artist's residency in Limousin. My nose is pressed to the glass, watching the rolling green pastures, old stone barns and fences, houses red with Virginia Creeper, and pink geraniums spilling out of window boxes.

I enter the French country house and find my room on the second floor. It has green shutters with no glass or screen to separate me from the smell of fresh-cut green grass and the flutter of aspen leaves.

I unpack and walk down the road, past the lake, through the old wooden arches to Villefavard for evening dinner.

Justine, Natalie's assistant, is orienting us. "Silence is observed at all times except when you are in class. Silence will be broken following breakfast next week on Monday. Tuesday is our field trip to the historic city of Limoges. Wednesday evening we return to the formal retreat and silence. I think that's it. Oh, and the basket by Natalie's chair is for questions."

Day 1

By 7:30 a.m. the next morning we are sitting in the zendo, all gathered for the same reasons: Zen and writing and the woman leading it.

Natalie greets us warmly. "Welcome. I know many of you have traveled from other continents. The travel alone is tiring, so be kind to yourselves." She turns to Justine and asks if we've been told about the wildflowers and the schedule, then continues. "When you arrange your wildflowers, just set them around the property. And remember, they're WILD flowers. If we see Dahlias in your arrangements we'll know you were raiding villagers' gardens."

We hear the church bell ring outside the zendo. Natalie tells us that it rings once on the half-hour and full on the hour—even during the night. We'll get used to it, she says; after a while we won't even notice it. "When the church bell rings, stop. Bring your attention back to the breath for however many rings. Just notice it and breathe."

Getting down to business, she lists the books we'll be studying: Paris France by Gertrude Stein on Friday; The Stranger by Albert Camus; Haiku Master Buson and Giovanni's Room by James Baldwin.

"And don't be reading anything else during the retreat—unless it's something really great! Let's sit."

The meditation bell rings and Natalie asks, "Does everyone have your sketchbooks? This is the first time I've done this so we are just going to try it and see what happens. Take your sketchbook and wander until you find a spot where you'd like to sit. Draw whatever is in front of you. We will meet back here in forty minutes."

I take up a position on the dock and draw my feet in the water.

I'd first noticed the desperate need to be perfect in pottery class back in the nineties. We were wedging clay, cutting it with a string, pounding it on the tables. I threw the clay on the wheel and cupped my hands around it, but instead of guiding it upward, the bottom of the clay spread like a crepe, and I was vibrating like an off-center washing machine.

"What makes you so special?' Dr. E, my therapist at the time, asked. "Why should you be able to create something perfect on your first try? Why do you get to skip being a beginner?"

We're back in the zendo.

"How was that?" Natalie asks.

We all agree we liked the drawing exercise.

"Lay your sketchbooks open in front of your seat and everyone just take a walk around the room and see what each of you has drawn." We move slowly around the room, completing the circle.

Natalie takes her seat. "Some of you are pretty good drawers, the only difference between you and me is I kept doing it."

Day 3

It's lunchtime. I drop a question into Natalie's basket.

So, I know during meditation we're to bring our minds back to the breath, but what do we do when we have all day and night in silence, with only the mind?

After lunch of a starter and hot entrée, followed by cheese and fruit plates, I take my notebook and sit in the courtyard to sketch the church steeple. This new practice is the doorway into a well of writing.

We settle in the zendo. Natalie is looking through slips of paper. "Where is that question. I saw it earlier ... here it is," she begins to read, "*So, I know during meditation...*"

My inner twelve-year-old wants to jump up and down. That's my question!

"Bring it back to the moment," Natalie continues, "If you are walking, feel your feet making contact with the floor or ground. If you are drawing, what is in front of you that you're drawing? Pay attention to the details." She pauses and surveys the room.

"This is a challenging retreat. It is not easy to be in silence for this long. Be kind to yourself. It takes a while for your mind to really land. Just try to watch your mind. You know, I even have these moments. This morning I woke and I thought what am I doing here? I have cancer. I should be home resting. I have medication to take. What am I doing in France teaching?"

"This is your opportunity to follow the mind ... to really get to know writer's mind."

Day 7

Natalie is preparing us to break silence. "The urge is to talk very fast and very loud because you have been in silence for so long. Just try to be aware of that and do your best to remain mindful of your speech. Listen for the church bell."

Despite the warnings, the dining room is a buzz with people's chatter.

We meet for evening meditation. Natalie is leading us through the village, slow walking.

As we pass the cornfield in relative silence, Natalie asks a writer to pick her an ear of corn. He walks through the ditch and breaks off two cobs. He goes on to explain that the corn is feedstock and not for human consumption. We all laugh as we see the farmers on an evening stroll heading toward us.

Natalie puts the ears of corn behind her back. The farmers are speaking in a French dialect rarely spoken. The adult son interprets for his parents. We all enjoy the conversation.

We continue, past the Brussels sprout farm, and through two small hamlets, the last of which is Le Solitude.

I break off from the group and go to bed early. Although I want to go to Limoges, I feel reluctant to lose this stillness.

The morning promises a warm autumn day. I pull a colorful dress from the closet, breaking from the dark colors of the zendo. I apply makeup, do my hair, and get ready to head toward the bus that will take us to the city.

The bus arrives as I step through the old wooden arch in Ville de Favard.

I hear the word clearly audible, but not spoken: "stay." I do as Dr. Wayne Dyer suggests, I suspend all doubt, and I follow the whisper.

"No problem," Justine says, clipboard in hand. "It's just you and Helen staying. I'll let the kitchen know."

Helen walks into the lounge as I am about to exit. "How are you feeling about today, Anneli? Do you wish to hold silence?" We agree we'll only break silence over lunch.

I kick off my sandals and begin slow walking. The sun is hot. I want to feel the pebbles bite the bottom of my bare feet. I want to connect with the earth.

I continue walking from hamlet to hamlet. Feeling the sun on my body, my feet on the ground, I listen to the birds, young French boys call "bonjour" from their yards, dogs bark, every now and then a little car zooms past me. A motorbike, a cow, a rooster, fields of sheep graze lazily.

The lake is to my left, when I come upon the frog. He is the size of my hand. His yellowish green body is motionless and his hind legs tangled, his eyes flash wildly. His bodily fluids are spilt on the pavement and create a dark circle around him.

"I am sorry for your suffering, frog. There is nothing more to do but allow death to come." I sit down on the roadside and share in its last breaths.

> *Frog lies*
> *On hot asphalt*
> *Legs broken*
> *Death is coming*

I enter the dining room. Helen is already there. I sit across from her as she twists her salad onto her fork.

"I get so tired of the thoughts," she says, "Oh Natalie likes me, oh Natalie hates me."

"You mean I'm not the only one?" I say, astounded. "I thought it was just me having those feelings. I mean, look at you, Helen. You and the others ... you're so solid."

"There is so much more going on here around us, Anneli. This retreat is about more than lessons in writing practice—these are lessons in learning how to live. At seventy-five, I'm still learning them. There's so many emotions surfacing and we are experiencing them each and every day. Someone reads and we feel jealousy or we feel that their writing is so much better than ours. Natalie calls on us in class and we feel like a million bucks. She calls on someone else and we feel ignored."

I smile. "It sounds childish doesn't it? But it's human emotion, raw, unedited, uncensored human emotion. It's the stuff we turn from, bury, refuse to see, anything to avoid the emotions that well up inside of us. Thank you, Helen. I've enjoyed our conversation more than you know."

Day 8

I am in the student lounge; the window is thrown open to the right of the writing desk, and I am aware of the sunshine. I have been writing for hours, oblivious to time and my surroundings. A flood of words and tears, I have a stack of over twenty-five pages on the desk beside me. Now I look up and gaze from person to person. Natalie and her long-term students and assistants all sit quietly nearby.

Later in the zendo we are preparing to return to silence. I'm sitting on my cushion with my eyes closed when I feel something poking my back. I turn and Natalie is sitting on my chair behind me, her legs crossed, with her big toe tapping my spine. I am warmed by her support of my deep dive.

Helen's hand is up and she is asked to read, our eyes meet for a moment across the zendo, and I settle in to listen to her writing.

Final Day

There's a mix of excitement and melancholy as we take part in activities. Several of us are serving our fellow students and Natalie at a formal tea ceremony before we have our final dinner together.

I sit in the courtyard and draw the tile rooftops. The young French kitchen maiden, round and juicy like a ripe peach, appears in the doorway. She rests the thick, heavy breadboard on her hip and slaps it with the palm of her hand. Sprays of flour dust rise and fall, settling on the red geraniums in weathered clay pots, set next to the firewood.

We gather for evening meditation, sitting once more overlooking the pasture, red cushions lined up on the grass, writers gathering together on benches. The sunset and painted skies above us leave us in silent astonishment.

People are gathered in the student lounge looking at Natalie's website. They're buying paintings and booking future retreats before they've even had a moment to check their schedules. We are all drunk on Natalie Goldberg.

I want to jump into the middle of it all, but instead I take a deep breath and I slip out the door. I walk back to Le Solitude alone in the dark. A full heart and a quiet mind.

ABOUT THE AUTHOR: Anneli grew up under the vast blue skies and golden wheat fields of the Canadian Prairies. The solitude of the country and the backdrop of nature nurtured an innate ability to slow down, observe the world, and use the gift of imagination. This contemplative approach continues today as Anneli begins to explore, with greater intention, the role of art in personal and collective freedom of expression. Anneli has followed a writing practice for more than twenty-five years. She can be found working in her expressive arts studio in Victoria, British Columbia, Canada.

Anneli Davey
Artist, Writer, Wayfinder Coach
annelidavey.com
annelidavey@gmail.com

Consciously Recognizing My Self

Tami Bulmash

I was thrilled when in 2001 I was accepted into a great drama program in London. Looking back, though, I think I just wanted an excuse to live there. I *loved* London. There was always something to do in this vibrant city. I could sit and draw elm trees in Hyde Park for hours, breathing in the sweetness of the rose garden; I could catch some jazz at Camden Town, walk aimlessly through Convent Gardens, ponder at the River Thames…and finish the day with some friends at the pub. There was never a shortage of places to see or people to meet.

In contrast to the art and freedom that lured me to the streets of London, drama school had a different appeal. It was intense and demanding. The days were long and filled to the brim. We had vocal coaches, dialect experts, stage combat, ballroom dance, film and radio technique, singing, movement classes, and the Alexander Technique.

The Alexander Technique is a method used to recognize undesired habits that interfere with the body's optimal functioning. It promotes ease and mobility in activity, which is why it is an effective tool for performers. However, the Alexander Technique isn't just limited to performers; it is widely used by people from all walks of life to alleviate body pain and improve posture.

Despite these benefits, the Alexander Technique remained an enigma to me. As I sat there with my classmates, observing each other as we moved and got into and out of a chair, I didn't see the point of any of it.

Yet, some of the feedback that I received from my

performances was that I moved awkwardly on stage. I'd never thought about how I moved before. I was never any good at dance or athletics, so I just accepted this was the way I was. The Alexander Technique was meant to help me move more fluidly on stage and Maya Galai, the Alexander Technique teacher who taught the class, suggested I take private lessons with a woman named Manoli Garcia-Saavedra. Meeting Manoli would become one of the defining moments of my life.

Manoli had a warm Mediterranean smile and a way that made me feel that anything I said was okay. She was the first person who *invited* me to find my *self*. I wasn't required *to do* anything; in fact, she didn't want me *to do* anything. She made me feel safe in this space to explore and make mistakes. Every time that I fell into the chair, she would help me find my way up. More significantly, Manoli helped me understand that I was using my self in ways that were literally bringing me down.

During one lesson, I explained to Manoli how hard it was for me to say "no" to people. I didn't want to disappoint them or let them down.

"Just try saying it once," she suggested.

That didn't sound too hard to do. So, I did it. And something incredible happened. After I said "no" once, it became a lot easier to say it again. What's more, when I said "no", I really meant it. This was a big breakthrough for me, for when I previously said "yes" to something I hadn't really meant—I was acting out of habit. I was beginning to understand how saying something that you mean strengthens the connection with your heart and soul.

This lesson would become a foundation in other aspects of my life. Once I recognized an undesired habit, I could resist it, and then try something new. It didn't always feel right—sometimes it felt unfamiliar or wrong—but the second that I tried something different, I allowed my self the opportunity to break a pattern.

Moving to Tel-Aviv in 2005 and enrolling in Shaike and Linda

Hermelin's Alexander Technique teacher training school, was the quintessential "trying something new" for me. Shaike is a renowned Master Alexander Technique teacher. He studied with Patrick MacDonald, who was one of the first students of the Technique's founder, F.M. Alexander. To this day, I feel blessed for the training I received. Over the next three years, Shaike and Linda would mentor and direct me with gentleness and compassion, setting me on a course to study, research, and teach the Alexander Technique and make it my passion.

Habits were a recurring topic during the course—not just the obvious ones like excessive eating, drinking, smoking, working, exercising, nail biting, et cetera, but those ones we barely notice, such as the excessive tension we hold in our bodies—all day, every day.

I was realizing what had been missing from my first Alexander Technique experience at drama school: I hadn't understood the importance of observation. I was watching my peers get into and out of a chair without paying attention to *how* they were doing it. Were they tightening their necks as they were getting up? Were they arching their backs as they sat? Or slouching as they collapsed into their chairs? Tightening, arching, and collapsing are all associated with putting undue tension on the musculoskeletal system.

Why is all of this even important? Well there are innumerable habits that we accrue through life. They show up in everything that we think, say, and do, usually in indirect ways that aren't even noticeable—especially to our self. Repeating these habits forms layers of tension that weigh on us and result in misuse of our bodies. Our physical posture is merely the manifestation of our thoughts, actions, and reactions.

Initially, I didn't recognize this in my self. I continued to react to the triggers around me. My thoughts were discombobulated. I constantly felt like I wasn't doing enough—I wasn't *good* enough.

With every thought came stress and tension. When we are stressed we hold tension and unknowingly tighten our necks, lock our jaw, and tense our shoulders and back. We have to-do lists and "shoulda woulda couldas" running through our heads throughout the day and coupled with work and responsibilities they act as a stimulus, a trigger. When triggered, we become over stimulated, or overworked, and then collapse into exhaustion, only to repeat the cycle all over again.

Thinking back to that first year of Alexander Technique training, I realize I was really a mess. Sometimes I would just cry, slowly releasing some of the cumbersome tension I wasn't even aware that I was holding on to. I felt very emotional and afraid of confronting my habits. There seemed to be so many of them! I will never forget something that Shaike, once told me. He said, "Anyone who thinks that they can make it through life without any help, is mistaken." What sage advice indeed.

I started paying attention to a habit that was becoming increasingly evident to me. It seemed like I had *to do* so much *all the time*. A fellow student named Dana once said to me, "Tami, have you ever thought of only giving eighty percent? Maybe your one-hundred percent is so much more than one-hundred percent that if you allowed yourself to just give eighty percent it would still be enough." What I heard for the first time in my life was that I had *permission* to do less. *Giving my self permission to not try so hard.* Now that was liberating!

I found many others who would also help me on my path. Roy Carmel, a wonderful acupuncturist in Israel, told me that according to Chinese Medicine, we are meant to experience *every* emotion once a day. The concept seemed both foreign and inherent. Instead of thinking that I always had to smile or be nice or "happy" I suddenly gave myself permission to be angry and sad—in front of others. Doesn't that make more sense anyway? Would we limit our self to only eating sweets every day or would we want to balance our palate by engaging in each flavor?

Years later, a friend and mentor named Wendy would tell me, "We teach what we need to learn." This truth really hit home. I became a teacher of the Alexander Technique because I needed to learn it for my self, first. And in every lesson that I teach, I continue to work on my self.

The Alexander Technique has been a part of my life for over seventeen years. What started as a required course in drama school became a way of life for me that promotes health and con-sciousness. Rather than perceiving habits as external or outside of the body, I now understand them to be unrecognized tension that disrupts the body's functioning. The repetition of habitual thoughts and behaviors leads to misuse of the body. If I tell my self, "I'm not good enough," I tighten and then constrict. Does that create space, openness, and fluidity in my body, or does it shrink and confine my sense of self?

There is also a scientific and practical relationship between posture and wellness. For example, the way we sit and hold our bodies has a direct correlation to our mood and well-being.[1] In today's technology centric-lifestyle, we spend most of our waking hours sitting down.[2] What's more, we are usually behind some type of screen when we sit, which further strains our cervical spine.[3] Sedentary lifestyles (which include excessive technology usage) are associated with several health conditions such as obesity,[4] asthma, diabetes, hypertension, coronary disease,[5] finger and wrist pain, vision and hearing impairment, and neck and back pain.[6] This is detrimental to adults, and more poignantly, to children's musculoskeletal health as well.[7]

What happens when we sit in front of a computer? Do we have a number of windows open? Are we surfing the net, listening to music, checking messages on our phone, drinking a cup of coffee, taking a bite of a sandwich...all while working? The number of stimuli we are responding to is mind-boggling, and it has consequences. It wreaks havoc on the body. It causes stimulus overload, which leads to tensing and tightening throughout our body. When this is coupled with the heavy musculoskeletal task of trying to balance our bodies in a sedentary position for eight to ten hours a day, the tension associated with our response to stimuli is also weighing. Is it any wonder why many people who sit down for the majority of their day complain of headaches, neck, shoulder, and back pain?

As we evolve we will continue to be exposed to a plethora of stimuli; however, we don't have to engage with or react to all of it. The key is to bring those habits into consciousness. By doing so, we free the space in our body, which allows our entire self to feel more balanced in every aspect of our lives.

When I discovered the Alexander Technique, I began to *feel* inside of my body. I was no longer just stuck in my head, but rather learned to include the space of my body from the neck down. In a way, I felt like my body woke up. I understood that the mind and body were not separate entities; previously thinking that they were, only underscored the imbalance in my use.

None of this happened overnight. I did a lot of work on my self to recognize and pause before reacting to a trigger. I allowed my self to make new choices. It meant saying "no" to habits that weighed me down and saying "yes" to new possibilities that brought me up. That doesn't mean that I don't have undesired habits. The difference now is that I know how to recognize them and choose not to engage.

People are drawn to the Alexander Technique for various reasons. Students come to me for lessons due to chronic pain, or because they want to improve their performance or posture. The Alexander Technique means something different to each of them. Many see it as a scientific method or therapy. Others see it as an educational tool for continued self-care. Some see it as a spiritual experience. I see it as all of those things, and I will add that for me, it was a journey to self-discovery that eventually led me to consciously recognizing my self.

ABOUT THE AUTHOR: Tami Bulmash has devoted the past seventeen years to the study, research, and teaching of the Alexander Technique. She holds undergraduate and graduate degrees rooted in the behavioral sciences, which have helped inform her approach to and understanding of human behavior. Tami has been a certified teacher of the Technique since 2009 and is a member of both the American Society for the Alexander Technique (AmSAT) and the Society of Teachers of the Alexander Technique (STAT). She is also the author of "iPosture: A Closer Look at the Lifestyle Practices of Schoolchildren." Tami lives and works in Melbourne, Florida.

Tami Bulmash
Body and Posture LLC
bodyandposture.com
tbulmash@yahoo.com
813-534-9219

Endnotes
1. Peper, E. Lin, I-M, & Harvey, R. (2017). Posture and mood: Implications and applications to therapy. Biofeedback.35(2), 42-48.
https://biofeedbackhealth.files.wordpress.com/2017/11/a-article-biof-45-02-42-48.pdf.
2. Matthews, Charles E. et al. "Amount of Time Spent in Sedentary Behaviors in the United States, 2003-2004." *American journal of epidemiology* 167.7 (2008): 875-881.
3. Hansraj, Kenneth K. "Assessment of stresses in the cervical spine caused by posture and position of the head." *Surgical Technology International* 25 (2014): 277-279.
4. Gilleard, W., and T. Smith. "Effect of obesity on posture and hip joint moments during a standing task, and trunk forward flexion motion." *International Journal of Obesity* 31, no. 2 (2007): 267-271.
5. DeMarco, Terri, and Ken Sidney. "Enhancing children's participation in physical activity." *Journal of School Health* 59, no. 8 (1989): 337-341.
6. Samakow, J.& Leibovich, L. "Here's What a Constantly Plugged-In Life is Doing to Kids' Bodies." *Huffingtonpost.com* (2013)
http://www.huffingtonpost.com/2013/10/17/teens-on-screens_n_4101758.html.
7. Bulmash, Tami "iPosture: A Closer Look at the Lifestyle Practices of Schoolchildren" *AmSAT Journal*, 13 (2018):32-37.

Removing the Sword
Mae Fox

I closed my eyes as Deanna placed her hands on my shoulders, internally bracing myself for the wave of emotion I knew would come. The heat moved from her hands to my very center, and tears I could not stop flowed silently down my face. She moved slowly and purposefully, her hands now on my sides, and quietly asked, "Mae, do I have your permission to remove this sword from your side?"

My eyes snapped open and looked into hers. *Are you serious?! I thought. What was she doing?!*

"Mae?" she asked, waiting for my consent. This was it. This was why I was here. The familiar tsunami threatened to overwhelm me, crashing and wiping out all sense of self and security. The ocean of grief swirled and howled beneath. I could continue to close a door of iron and steel upon it, anesthetize my heart, and numb my soul, or I could ask for help. I felt naked.

"Sure…"

Deanna leaned forward, reaching for and grabbing an imaginary sword, and then slowly pulled it from my body. Awestruck, I could *feel* it coming out. Every. Single. Inch.

My sister had died. Not, just my sister, my TWIN. The other half of myself. Jean and I were only seventeen years old, and consumed by our plans for the future. We were talking about going to college, what cars we wanted; careers, marriage, babies, and adventure. We would do it all together—we were a couple. We came into this life together, and the plan was always to BE TWINS—forever.

But I was alone. My partner was gone. Shock rippled through my family and through my town. In the days and weeks that followed, I dared not completely feel that loss. Weeks turned into months, then months into years.

And so I existed. I convinced myself and everyone around me that I was okay. I was strong. I laughed and worked and socialized. I went to parties and had relationships. I had family and tons of friends. But I was not whole. Part of me was lost, and, even if I allowed myself to recognize it, it was impossible for me to reach out for help.

Who am I, if not a twin? Will I ever feel whole?

I was among so many, but I felt totally isolated. That loneliness had become excruciating.

To be vulnerable was to feel, and to feel was to feel ALL of it. The pain, the loss, the helplessness. Betrayal, anger, guilt, and fear. My body was heavy with the weight of it.

But there was also something else—an almost too-beautiful knowing I carried but never gave light to: the night my sister transitioned, she came to me. She asked me what was happening, and I hugged her. Then she disappeared. She visited others whom she loved as well. There is so much more to this world, to our souls and energy, to OURSELVES than what happens in this lifetime. Our energy is powerful. It is singular and connected, one and part of the Whole. It is love and abundance and grace and joy.

Cradled within me was a voice that said, *You are more.* I knew this. I also knew deep down that Jean was not truly gone. But at the same time, the pain of her departure was simply too great to be borne. I cut myself off from that suffocating emptiness just so I could breathe, but, in doing so, the brightness of my entire spirit was also dimmed. I became a spectator in my own life: things happened *TO* me. Although my shell was hard, inside I felt broken, crumbling, and without purpose.

My young family would be the catalyst for healing. I remember sitting on my couch, watching my beautiful little daughter play, and suddenly thinking, *"I'm not happy."* I didn't know why I couldn't fully engage to really feel her light and joy, but I knew it was time to figure it out. I was tired of allowing myself to be putty in some hypothetical cosmic hands. However, painful it was, I had to take the risk; my husband and daughter deserved it. *I deserved it.*

I started working regularly with a grief counselor. She was young and funny. I felt safe there, and I liked her. One day, I was curled up in the familiar brown loveseat when she settled in, looked at me thoughtfully, and asked, "Hey Mae, what do you think about some anger management classes?" But I wasn't angry. She'd missed the mark on this one. It must have been all over my face because she explained, "I know you're not aggressive, but I feel it will help you." We had spent the entire summer working together. I trusted her, so I agreed. It was in that class that I would first meet Deanna, who was serving as facilitator.

I soon found myself standing before a very large man; we were to "square off," and yell at each other to release pent-up emotions. My whole body was quivering. He barked, loud, strong, and sharp. My response was weak and shaky. I was uncomfortable and nervous and scared… and I was falling apart. My breaking point was imminent but I was powerless to rein it back in. The lump in my throat grew and my eyes began to burn. I could feel the words trapped in my throat but I just couldn't let them out. My knees buckled as I crumbled to the floor where I cried, my hands hiding my face.

Anger wasn't my issue—I was totally incapable of expressing myself. Actually, I was afraid of what would happen if I tried. *What if there is no bottom? What if it's just too deep? What if I get stuck or sucked into the darkness?* I have always swallowed the emotion down to the point that, when it did flow up to be expressed, I had no idea how to open up and let it out.

After class, Deanna spoke with me about her energy work. It was new to me, but I was ready, ready to stop hiding from myself.

We began working together, both privately and within a women's group. I began to open up, to acknowledge and talk about my feelings. Something was unlocking within me. I found myself in a new place emotionally, mentally, and even physically. The possibility of life being bigger than I had ever imagined was freeing. I became an active member in my own journey and healing. The more I learned about energy, the stronger I felt. Hope flowed through me. I could breathe easier. Deanna had created a Sacred Space, where I felt safe enough to allow that "sword" to be removed from my side.

Fate has a funny way of putting us in situations, and I found myself taking classes with Deanna and other teachers of energy healing. Each one came with a certificate to practice; I came armed with a thirst for healing. Life gave me an opportunity to move in a different direction, when the company I was working for dissolved. Out of a job and unsure what I wanted to do I went for personality testing. The result, hands-down, was NURSING. This was interesting because I knew I could not legally have a healing practice without a license to put my hands on people. I had to do it. Self-doubt and fears floated to the surface but I kept them at bay with all of the tools I gained and began a career in the medical field. It has been eighteen years, and I have strengthened my practice by integrating the certifications in Reiki, Hands of Light, Wellness/Spiritual coaching, and hypnosis. My numbness was replaced by excitement and passion for my life and this work. I felt my whole spirit come alive

My healing has been a journey, one that has taken time and work. That journey continues to this day, and because I know that no price can be placed on the safety a sacred space allows, I created

A-Mae-Zing Mind Body Soul Center. Healing and unlocking of doors becomes easier when we are in the proper setting, and my clients feel it as soon as they walk inside.

We all experience heartache and trauma in this life, and I have learned that how we respond directly impacts our happiness. When my perspective shifted from that of a victim of some cruel plotline, into the knowing that I co-create my life, self-empowerment was the lesson I learned. This is possible for all of us. We can't control every outcome, but when we hold on to the faith and understanding that our single lives have real purpose, our spirits open, unfold, and blossom. We become.

At the *A-Mae-Zing Mind Body Soul Center*, every healing plan is tailored to the client. Everybody's wounds are their own, and pain is seated in different ways and in different places. When someone comes to me, I create a healing program specifically and uniquely to that person to ensure the most effective treatment. This creates an experience of deep change, working at the root of every issue.

I also facilitate a Women's Group as a safe, supportive, and confidential space for members to explore their feelings and heal in a community of like-minded people. I know and have experienced the power of these groups. That is why I hold space for them.

Writing a new chapter is how we use our experiences to grow and keep us moving forward instead of drowning. This is the essence of resilience: Our thoughts are tools for building our spirit up. That is what I had to learn, what I continue to practice for an even better tomorrow. By embracing a resilient perspective, we can stay buoyant. We can bring a lightness to stressors and painful experiences by challenging our choice of response. Will I become/remain a victim, or will I reassess/shift my perspective? There is magic in such a shift; I have seen it as a nurse, and as a hypnotist. Hypnosis releases my clients from their pain. It is like zooming out from the micro-shot of their own life, revealing larger possibilities. The healing is deep and life-changing. When I combine my medical experience, energetic healing, and hypnosis knowledge, A-Mae-Zing things happen—not only for my clients, but also for me.

For too long I was paralyzed by the fear of my own pain. Today, I am brave enough to sit with it. I trust myself to truly *feel*; I embrace the whole rainbow of emotions—which includes profound joy—and I entrust myself to the entire experience, to live in full-color. It is not the life Jean and I envisioned so many years ago, but I know now that in helping others to heal, I am fulfilling my purpose. I am Whole.

ABOUT THE AUTHOR: Mae Fox is a Registered Nurse, hypnotist, energy healer, and wellness coach based in the Finger Lakes region of New York. Her passion for self-healing, coupled with her innate ability to help others move from self-judgement to self-empowerment, led her to create A-Mae-Zing Mind Body Soul Center. There, her clients find a safe, sacred space in which they can heal past wounds and discover their individual paths to Wholeness. Mae is a speaker on Resilience for the medical community and public, and a board member of both the Professional Women of the Finger Lakes and Business Improvement Development for City of Canandaigua.

Mae Fox
A-Mae-Zing Mind Body Soul Center
A-Mae-Zing.com or MaeFox.com
amaezingcenter@gmail.com
585-880-6012

Spreading My Wings
Robin Eagle Sage

I remember as a child cringing at the idea of hugging or kissing anyone. I would rather have crawled into a hole and die than touch another person. It was only in the presence of animals that my shyness and sensitivity were alleviated. I could trust them. They would never hurt me the way people had. I was safe.

When I was young, my free time was spent cantering down the streets of New York City with Tiger, my enormous Great Dane. What I really wanted was a horse. In fact, I wholeheartedly believed I had been one in a past life. But since a horse would not fit into our apartment, I settled for a large dog. Ironically, people often asked if Tiger was a horse and if I rode her. At first the line was funny, but I quickly grew tired of it. I couldn't believe how childish adults were. I was never going to understand the two-legged race. Of course, I secretly wished I could ride my Great Dane and gallop like the wind across the mountains to the sea.

I never lost sight of my dream even though my mother assured me I could not have a horse in Manhattan. She was a single mother working multiple jobs just to make ends meet. Nonetheless, I spent countless hours lying in bed dreaming of taming a wild mustang. In my vision a white horse galloped through the tall grass at top speed as I effortlessly ran alongside it and jumped onto its back with the stealth of an Indian. There was no need for a saddle or bridal, as we communicated telepathically as one. We were united body, mind, and soul!

My New York doorman gave me countless racehorse magazines and I pasted photos of equine champions onto my bedroom walls from corner to corner. I wanted to become a jockey and race like the wind like in my vision. Imagine my surprise when I learned the first female jockey to win a major race in the United States was named Robyne Smith—so close to my own name! This could not have been a coincidence.

One day when I was eleven years old my mother told me my father was moving to Malibu, California and asked if I would like to move there with him. The deciding factor came when I asked my father if I could have a horse and he said yes! Little did I know I had been manifesting a horse all along. My bedroom walls that were filled with pictures of horses had actually been a gigantic vision board and my love for all things equine ignited a powerful emotion the Universe could not deny.

I soon found myself in horse heaven. I had a show jumper at the barn, my stepmom's horse in the backyard, and my friend's pony to boot. Before I knew it, I had become the Indian I dreamed of, galloping bareback over the mountains to reach the sea.

Several years later, after graduating from college, I found myself thrown onto the streets without financial support or any viable career. How was I going to make money with a Political Science degree? Why had I chosen to study that? I didn't even like watching the news. Why hadn't I followed my passions and gone to a horse-training school?

I took a job in a pet store doing the only thing I knew how to do: love and care for animals. The pay was minimal and I remember the worried look on my stepmother's face when I told her I would never take a job I didn't love with all my heart and soul. For years I lived below the poverty level, yet I never doubted following my heart. Little did I know at the time, my spirit was following a perfect trajectory.

One sunny day while taking a walk in Berkeley, my mother and I saw balloons on the street for a psychic fair. She suggested we go inside to take a look. That curiosity led to an energy reading with an intriguing and accurate woman whose eyes flickered as she spoke. My mouth dropped when I saw healers running their hands through the air around people's bodies. I was told it was their "auric field" and it could be cleansed to create greater health. Mesmerized, I wanted to know everything possible on the subject. As soon as I realized anyone could learn to read and heal energy I signed up for all the classes possible!

One day at clairvoyant school, our "readee" (or person we practice giving a reading to) was late and we began reading her energy before she arrived. Our teacher referred to our absent readee as a woman, however, when I looked at "her" energy I clearly saw it was a man. Should I say something and defy my teacher? What if I was wrong? I painstakingly offered that I thought it was a man who was scheduled to come for a reading. My teacher looked at the roster and confirmed indeed it was a man. When the man arrived for his reading my teacher asked me to be the lead reader, which I had never done before. Shy and lacking confidence, I told her no, that I was not ready to lead the group. I was afraid I would make a fool of myself! Fortunately, my teacher refused to take no for an answer, and with everyone's encouragement I slid into the center chair.

Unbelievably, I had found a world of spirit I understood and was actually good at. This world involved having compassion for people and a great deal of heart. Readees often cried during their sessions as they felt heard, seen, and understood, sometimes for the first time, on a spiritual level. We readers often sobbed after the readings as our own hearts dismantled challenges and similar wounds that were reflected back at us from our practice clients.

As my classmates chatted away during our group readings, it was me who would drop the bomb and instigate depth. It was the shy and quiet me who skipped the small talk and offered, "You have 'such and such' issue because you were raped and have not yet healed from it." My co-readers would gasp in shock and I could almost hear their hearts beating. Was I right? Had I defied all Gods? Would I be punished and sent to purgatory? After the reading had ended and others dispersed, the readee would inevitably make their way toward me and whisper into my ear that I was correct. This built my confidence. This built my life. This built my world. It allowed my wings to spread and I began to have faith in humanity.

I studied world religion in college, yet nothing gave me the answers to life and death until I discovered energy reading. I learned to meditate, answer my own questions clairvoyantly, and become my own Guru. I was becoming empowered and healing was happening at a quick clip. My wings were beginning to spread and I felt a freedom and clarity I had never before experienced. Life was beginning to make sense. Why we are here, where we are going, our purpose, our plan, our pain, and our chosen family. It was finally coming together.

As a child I often had vivid memories of being part of the Apache tribe. Now I understood the visions were coming from a past life. I wasn't crazy after all, I was psychic. I was so excited I wanted to shout out to the world! I wanted everyone to experience the peace I had found. I wanted everyone to know that anyone can learn to read energy and heal their wounds, such as the way I had healed my self-induced solitude. I wanted to share this skill with the world.

In 1999 I began my private practice as a medical intuitive healer. Soon afterward I opened a school of energy reading and healing called the Sage School of Light. It was a dream come true, yet I still had more to learn about sustaining a business. My financial struggles did not deter me from my goals. In fact, they pushed me to become more business and tech savvy, and more importantly, to listen closely to the messages I was receiving from Spirit. In 2016 my guidance told me to raise my hourly rate. I did so even though I was fearful no one would pay such a high price. The advice turned out to be on point and it ushered in an abundant business. Finally I had claimed my right to be a successful healer.

The Sage School of Light is thriving to this day, with a two-and-a-half-year Empowerment Program. It covers fourteen levels of energy reading and healing including: meditation, chakras, spirit guides, past lives, animal communication, relationships, finances, medical intuition, channeling, and so much more. In fact, the Sage School of Light may be the most in-depth intuitive program in the world today.

Because I learned marketing and business skills the hard way, I make a point to incorporate these fundamentals into the Empowerment Program from the get-go. This includes creating exposure, passive income, and how to become an expert in the field of energy medicine. This way my students will enjoy their rightful abundance while serving as light workers helping to raise the vibration of the planet. I feel blessed that my trials and tribulations have turned into experiential wisdom that will benefit my students in the making of many successful healing practices to come. Most importantly, I teach my students that all things are possible when following one's heart.

My journey of love and light was only the beginning. A couple of years ago I had an epiphany while watching Heartland, a show about a woman who trains horses using gentle and loving techniques. Why was I not training horses? I had been so caught up in helping others I had forgotten my own dreams! I got off the couch and got onto Craigslist where I immediately found a job training horses in Colorado.

After a year of successful horse training, my angels guided me to Madison Shambaugh, otherwise known as "Mustang Maddy," the foremost leader in wild mustang gentling. I enrolled in her weeklong training with six participants who would gentle six wild mustangs who had never before been touched by humans! On Day One, the mustangs were terrified and tried to jump over seven-foot fences to escape. By Day Seven we were petting them as they followed us around like trusting puppies. It was a highly emotional and life-altering experience. It was the epitome of my deepest childhood dreams.

The purpose of energy work is to enable our deepest desires to come true, whether a relationship, finances, health, or anything else. My next dream is to manifest land in Sedona, Arizona where I can gentle and re-home mustangs to save them from slaughter. Over 45,000 of these wild, beautiful creatures have been captured by the U.S. Bureau of Land Management and are being held in tight holding pens today. Many of the mustangs who do not sell in auctions will be sold to kill buyers. This is happening right under our noses. These powerful mustangs, the symbol of American freedom, deserve to be liberated just as we do. After all, isn't that the American dream?

My goal is to create a center called Spirit of the Mustangs. It will be a safe haven for mustangs that combines the healing of horses and people. Courses will be taught on mustang gentling, intuitive development, energy healing, and animal communication. I will specialize in training girls and women unique skills that directly translate into definable jobs, enriching their lives both financially and personally.

There is not a shadow of a doubt I will achieve this goal. I now wholeheartedly believe in myself—and the power of the Universe—to manifest the conditions needed for this dream. I need only to look back on my life, with all of its miracles, to know this is true.

ABOUT THE AUTHOR: Robin Eagle Sage is a medical intuitive, healer, clairvoyant reader, channel, teacher, and author. Robin serves clients the world over through private energy readings and healings via phone and Skype. She is also the founder of Sage School of Light and teaches weekly classes on energy reading and healing (including medical intuition) in a small group conference-call. She is the author of the book, "The Financial Alchemist," and creator of the CD, "Soul Love," as well as three audio meditations: "Love and Joy," "Releasing Stress and Anxiety", and "Financial Success and Abundance." When she is not helping people achieve their dreams, Robin is indulging her other passion: gentling wild mustangs.

Robin Eagle Sage - Making Your Dreams Come True!
Medical Intuitive and owner of Sage School of Light
MedicalIntuitiveTraining.com
info@RobinEagleSage.com
808-268-8501

A Natural Woman
Kathy Sipple

"Our true nature is like a precious jewel: although it may be temporarily buried in mud, it remains completely brilliant and unaffected. We simply have to uncover it." ~ Pema Chodron

A Gift from the Sea

It's June 1992. Anticipating a celebration of my one-year wedding anniversary on the 15th, I instead spend that day moving in with the roommate I'd found in the classifieds after my husband announces he no longer loves me and wants a divorce. On June 26th I turn 26, which, as a well-meaning friend explains is my "golden birthday"—the year your age matches the date. When she says this is a sign of good things to come, I want to believe her, and to be honest, I have every reason to. Until recently, my life has gone pretty well and according to plan—great childhood, graduation from a top university, a job I enjoyed, marrying the man I loved at a big Catholic wedding with all our friends and family present. I used to feel like the golden girl; now everything I consider sacred and have worked so hard to build has been torn apart. I feel broken.

I am numb and it's hard to focus at work. I need a break and some perspective. A true Cancerian woman, I love water and decide on a beach vacation. I cry during much of my thousand-mile drive to North Carolina's Outer Banks from my Midwest home and arrive exhausted and weepy.

I settle into a beach chair and stare at the ocean, pondering the dissolution of my marriage and the life I had envisioned. I am tired of this sad heaviness. The blue sky and the gentle waves beckon me to rise and be cleansed. With each step into the cool water, I release confusion, hurt, shame, jealousy and anger, and let it wash away with the tide. I splash the salty water on my tear-crusted face and let my own body's salt water mingle with the waters of the Atlantic.

Refreshed and tingly from my immersion, I return to my chair and open my newly purchased writing tablet. The dramatic dynamics of my marriage had left me always reacting to my husband rather than initiating much on my own. Washed of that responsibility, I am ready to turn that focus on myself instead. I begin to write what I want my new life to look like ...

First I concentrate on the basics, the creature comforts. I'd like an apartment of my own and eventually my own house. A new car. A dog. I need to start saving for my retirement. Though I like my job, it doesn't pay well or offer any room for advancement, so I probably need to update my resume. I want to go back to school, to study what I'm not sure but I've always loved learning. I want to travel more—I've never been out of the country except to Canada. Eventually, I want to start dating again and get married... Okay, that would be my five-year plan, then. It felt manageable.

"Essentials to happiness in this life are something to do, something to love, and something to hope for." ~ *Hector Garcia Puigcerver, Ikigai: The Japanese Secret to a Long and Happy Life*

I feel at peace, believing now that all will be well. I close my eyes and listen to the gentle lapping of the waves on the beach. In this relaxed state, I see a vision of myself in the future, at about sixty years of age. It seems quite natural, with rich detail, as if I am watching a movie. I have never experienced anything like this before. I watch the scene with rapt attention.

I look older—my blond hair had turned completely gray, but

my blue eyes looked the same though wiser and happier! My cheeks are flushed pink from a recent winter hike where I had guided a group through the nearby woods next to a lake. The group is now gathered around a fireplace and enjoying the healthy food I have prepared for them and listen attentively to me talking to them about healing. I know these people have come from near and far to learn from me how to connect with nature and with food in a new and healing way.

I wake refreshed, excited, and eager to commit my vision to paper in my journal. What my subconscious saw felt very real, though as yet I had absolutely no idea how this vision would become reality.

"What do you want to be when you grow up?" The question had always irked me because I had so many interests. During junior high school career day, I remember choosing landscape architect, marine biologist, and doctor. I had no idea what to call future me's profession, but it had aspects of all of those! I now knew what I wanted to be when I grew up! Now, to figure out how…

I keep that journal and refer to it frequently. The power of those words and intentions are powerful! Within four months I land a new job, with a higher salary as well as a retirement savings plan. A few months later, I find a great new apartment in a converted mansion with high ceilings and a fireplace. I get a sporty new little red convertible. I take trips to Mexico, Italy, France, Monaco, and go on a Caribbean cruise. A few years later, I have saved enough for a downpayment on a house; I look at only one place—it is perfect for me and I buy it. I begin to date again and meet some nice guys, but no one serious.

It's June 1997, almost the end of my five-year plan, and without love my other successes feel hollow. I'm grateful for everything I have experienced, but how does this connect me to my vision of the old woman in the woods? I am out of clues and don't know where to turn to get back on track. A friend recommends I see a psychic called Victor. I have seen therapists and am all for self-help books, but a psychic? This is out of my comfort zone and not something I believe in. I appreciate my friend's concern but balk at the suggestion. The next day my friend hands me an appointment card for a session with Victor. "If you want to cancel, of course, you can do that. But you shouldn't," she advised. "He can help you."

Still skeptical, but curious, I go. I enter a quiet bookstore I had never noticed before. It's after hours and all is quiet. We are alone and sit at a small table. Victor asks me to write my name and birthday on a piece of paper on the table in front of us and then he tunes into my heart chakra and begins to "read" information about me. He tells me I am an old soul, one of the oldest. He starts to tell me about a past life metaphor from 10,000 years ago and I get antsy and impatient. I don't understand how this will lead me to love or to becoming the Old Woman in the Woods, and though I don't mention anything about my vision I do let him know I'm more interested in concrete steps in *this* lifetime, like where to find love and also career advice.

Victor spends a few minutes telling me it is often useful to understand past lives, but I am uncharacteristically insistent. I now believe he can help me, but feel that time is of the essence. He refocuses and says he sees me meeting someone soon—a big, tall guy at a gathering of friends in the north woods and that there would be fireworks (literal fireworks). It may be the 4th of July. That's in just a few weeks, I think. I'll be alert! Nearing the end of our session, I ask if he has any insights about a career. He asks if I have considered working in the tradeshow industry. That seems oddly specific, I think. And no, I have never given a single thought to it. I don't know anyone in that field and I don't see how it's connected to the Old Woman in the Woods vision either. He advises me to remain open to what he has said and reminds me that I always have free will to choose my path.

"When will all of this happen?" I ask. "How will I know it's him?"

"Soon," he said, "You'll know."

Weeks later, I attend a friend's summer wedding hundreds of miles from my home near the shores of Lake Michigan. A tall, dark man sits down next to me; he is also alone. His name is John. He tells me he owns a trade show exhibit company! After the wedding, he is headed to his cabin on a lake in Northern Michigan and would I like to join him, along with a house full of family and friends?

It is an unusual week-long first "date" to say the least! We go fishing, enjoy hikes, and cook dinners together. I feel like one of the family right away. In the evenings we roast marshmallows and tell stories around the fire. And fireworks, lots of fireworks! We date long distance for several years and at last, we marry. This time it's all about substance and not at all about impressing anyone. We "elope" to the Northwoods of Wisconsin and wed underneath a canopy of snow-tipped trees with our black Labrador retriever walking me down the "aisle."

Now I'm no longer doubtful
Of what I'm living for
'Cause you make me feel
You make me feel
You make me feel like a natural woman (woman)
~ Aretha Franklin

I keep working at my regular job as Marketing Director at John's trade show exhibit company, and in my spare time I take classes and read books I feel bring me closer to the woman I saw myself becoming. I study herbalism, wild edibles, Reiki, massage, permaculture, metaphysics. I learn to make bread. I learn to grow vegetables and make compost. I spend more and more time in nature, especially in the woods near the Indiana Dunes on the South Shore of Lake Michigan where we now live.

As I spend more and more time in nature, an interesting thing happens. The forest begins to speak to me. I have one particular large Oak tree I hug often and it sometimes gives me messages. Once the tree's message was "Come, Unity. Community." Beautiful! I had never thought to break down the word community that way before on my own, so I am giving the tree credit. Another time the tree asked me to partner with it to bring "Bear Medicine" from the forest into the world, which leads me down an exciting path of discovery. Another time the tree "suggested" I study Shinrin-yoku, a term that means "taking in the forest atmosphere" or "forest bathing" in Japanese developed in the 1980s.

I finally find a Shinrin-yoku course that is perfect for me and I finally feel future me within reach. I turn fifty-two and decide to stop getting my hair colored and embrace my silvers since that's what my future self looks like. I'm ready to merge with her!

On our fifteen-year anniversary, John gives me an anniversary card that says, "I will love you on days when you're perfect in my eyes, and days when I wonder why you do the things you do." I'm grateful he supports my path toward wholeness because it certainly must look circuitous from the outside!

My journey is far from over; rather, it is a lifelong treasure hunt with much joyful exploration along the way. I have learned much since beginning on this path twenty years ago and I know I have much to learn ahead of me. One thing is never in doubt: the process of becoming who I really am is the greatest gift I could ever give myself.

ABOUT THE AUTHOR: Kathy Sipple resides just outside of Chicago near the Indiana Dunes with her husband John and their black Labrador retrievers, Bodhi and Pema. She is a frequent keynote speaker and trainer and host of 219 GreenConnect podcast. She holds a B.A. in Economics from the University of Michigan and is a member of Mensa. She won a Golden Innovator Award from Barbara Marx Hubbard and Conscious Evolutionaries Chicagoland for her empowering and groundbreaking work in social media. Sipple's career continues to evolve; however, she continues to work online with clients everywhere to provide social media strategy, training, and coaching while she pursues a Shinrin-yoku guide certification.

Kathy Sipple
Inspired life and business, guided by nature
kathysipple.com
kasipple@gmail.com
219-405-9482

About the Authors

Are you inspired by the stories in this book?
Let the authors know.

See the contact information at the end of each chapter
and reach out to them.

They'd love to hear from you!

Author Rights & Disclaimer

Each author in this book retains the copyright and all inherent rights to their individual chapter. Their stories are printed herein with each author's permission.

Each author is responsible for the individual opinions expressed through their words. Powerful You! Publishing bears no responsibility for the content of the stories by these authors.

Acknowledgements & Gratitude

OUR GRATITUDE bubbles over to all who have come together to lift the world with us to a space of heart, soul, love and possibility. There are many beautiful souls who we gratefully call our tribe who contribute their guidance, expertise, love, and support to us.

To our authors, we respect, appreciate, and love you. You've stepped forward to shine your light through your stories and you have done so with beauty, grace, and courage. As your words show, you are strong, determined, and resilient, as well as humble, gentle, and open. You provide a beautiful example for those facing challenges, and we're truly honored to share this journey with you. We thank you for stepping so intentionally and fully forth so that others may learn and grow from you. You are each a beautiful symbol for a life lived from the heart & soul.

Our editor Dana Micheli who knows the deep questions to ask to get to the heart and soul of each story. We love, appreciate, and enjoy you.

Our training team, AmondaRose Igoe, Kathy Sipple, and Linda Albright—your caring hearts and vast expertise light the way for our authors. We love, honor, and appreciate each of you!

Marcy Neumann, our dear friend and enlightened spirit—Your words are a masterpiece of inspired truth to light the way for individuals to shift and shine from the heart.

Our friends and families, we love you! Your loving support of our ventures and dreams continue to encourage us to faithfully pursue our passion and vision for life.

Above all, we are grateful for the Divine Spirit that flows through us each day providing blessings, lessons, and opportunities for growth, peace, and expansion.

Namaste` and Blessings, Love and Gratitude,
Sue Urda and Kathy Fyler

About Sue Urda and Kathy Fyler

Sue and Kathy have been friends for 28 years and business partners since 1994. They have received many awards and accolades for their businesses over the years and continue to love the work they do and the people they do it with. As publishers, they are honored to help people share their stories, passions, and lessons.

Their pride and joy is Powerful You!, which they know is a gift from Spirit. They love traveling the country producing meetings and tour events to gather women for personal development, business insights, and spiritual growth. Their greatest pleasure comes through connecting with the many inspiring and extraordinary women who are a part of their network.

The strength of their partnership lies in their deep respect, love, and understanding of one another as well as their complementary skills and knowledge. Kathy is a technology enthusiast and free-thinker. Sue is an author and speaker with a love of creative undertakings. Their honor for and admiration of each other are boundless.

Together their energies combine to feed the flames of countless women who are seeking truth, empowerment, joy, peace, and connection with themselves, their own spirits, and other women.

Connect with Sue and Kathy:
Powerful You! Inc.
239-280-0111
info@powerfulyou.com
PowerfulYou.com
PowerfulYouPublishing.com
SueUrda.com

Powerful You!
Women's Circles & Online Network
Connecting & Empowering Women

OUR MISSION is to empower women to find their inner wisdom, follow their passion, and live rich, authentic lives. It is our purpose and responsibility to raise the vibration of people and the planet.

Powerful You! is founded upon the belief that women are powerful creators, passionate and compassionate leaders, and the heart and backbone of our world's homes, businesses, and communities.

We designed our Women's Circles and online network to gather women and provide lessons and opportunities for growth in all areas of life: personal, spiritual, physical, emotional, relational, business, and financial. All aspects contribute to the wholeness of each woman, and each woman contributes to the wholeness of our global community.

Powerful You! was founded in January 2005 and continues to evolve. Our monthly gatherings provide a space for *real connections*, friendships, and collaborative, inspired networking. We know lasting relationships are built through open and meaningful conversation, so we've designed our gatherings to include introductions, monthly lessons and discussions, tips for growth, presentations, and gratitude shares.

**JOIN OR START A CIRCLE
IN YOUR COMMUNITY**

Follow us online:
Twitter: @powerfulyou
facebook.com/powerfulyou

powerfulyou.com

Are You Called to be an Author?

If you're like most people, you may find the prospect of writing a book daunting. Where to begin? How to proceed? No worries! We're here to help.

Whether you choose to write your own book, contribute to an anthology, or be part of our Wisdom & Insights book series of individually-authored teaching guides using our QuickPublish Formula^{TM}, we'll be your guiding light, professional consultant, and enthusiastic supporter. If you see yourself as an author partnering with a publishing company who has your best interest at heart and with the expertise to back it up, we're the publisher for you.

We provide personalized guidance through the writing and editing process. We offer complete publishing packages and our service is designed for a personal and optimal authoring experience.

We are committed to helping individuals express their voices and shine their lights into the world. Are you ready to start your journey as an author? Do it with Powerful You! Publishing.

Powerful You! Publishing
239-280-0111
powerfulyoupublishing.com

Anthology Books

Empowering Transformations for Women

Women Living Consciously

Journey to Joy

Pathways to Vibrant Health & Well-Being

Women Living Consciously Book II

Healthy, Abundant, and Wise

Keys to Conscious Business Growth

The Gifts of Grace & Gratitude

Heal Thy Self

Empower Your Life

Other Books

Powerful Intentions, Everyday Gratitude - Books I & II

Let Me Walk the Journey with You

Medicine Jewelry – Working with Rock People

Led By Purpose

Divinely Fit

A Journey Back to Restoration

About Marcy Neumann

Marcy Neumann, Rev., RN, CHT, RMT is a professional Energy Healer, Integrative Intuitive Counselor, Spiritualist Minister, Certified Hypnotherapist and Reiki Master. Marcy is also a published author, creator of award-winning manifestation and healing products and public speaker.

For over 45 years Marcy's professional journey has been guided by her own teachings of energy healing and manifestation in her own propriety process known as Heart*Shifting*. It's a recalibration of energy leading to Self Love.

This energy shifting leads to an unshakeable, solid, lasting Self Love that not only gets you the life you want, you deserve, and you were born to live ... but it sustains you and keeps you centered and coming back to your authentic self.

As far as making lasting changes, it is considered among the leading energy shifting and healing processes out today.

Marcy is living proof that Heart*Shifting* does work.

To learn more about Marcy, her programs, coaching & products, visit her website and connect with her on social media:

Website: heartshiftcoach.com
Facebook: facebook.com/HeartShiftCoach
Twitter: twitter.com/HeartShiftCoach
Instagram: instagram.com/HeartShiftCoach
Google +: plus.google.com/106365988716317627233
YouTube: youtube.com/channel/UCnbakILWQJXgTVzDaaHEllQ

May Your Heart Be Open.

May Your Soul Be Expansive.